CW01664937

BR DIARY 1978-1985

BR DIARY 1978-1985

LOND

IAN ALLAN LTD

John Glover

First published 1985

ISBN 0 7110 1522 8

All rights reserved. No part of this book may be reproduced or transmitted in any form or by any means, electronic or mechanical, including photocopying, recording or by any information storage and retrieval system, without permission from the Publisher in writing.

© Ian Allan Ltd, 1985

Published by Ian Allan Ltd, Shepperton, Surrey; and printed by Ian Allan Printing Ltd at their works at Coombelands in Runnymede, England

Previous page:
The 'Night Ferry', with its through Wagon-Lits sleeping car services to Paris and Brussels routed via the Dover-Dunkirk train ferry, was at last declared an anachronism and withdrawn on 31 October 1980. Electro-diesel No 73.141 awaits departure from Victoria. The train's demise brought to an end through rail passenger services to the European mainland. *Brian Morrison*

Cover, top:
British Rail promotional literature. *BR*

Cover, bottom:
An HST seen leaving King's Cross. *John Glover*

Below:
In summer, No 40.096 passes Blea Moor with a down freight before the loops were removed. *Les Nixon*

Contents

Preface 6

1978

Sir Peter Parker's railway 8
The Return of Freightliners 10
Merseyrail Complete 12
Level Crossing protection 14
GN Suburban electrification 16

1979

European Rail Performance 22
Passenger Marketing 24
Scottish Achievements 26
Centenary of Train Catering 28
EMU Refurbishing 30

1980

London and South East Commuters 36
Inter-City 1980 38
Glasgow Underground 40
Wagonload Freight 42
The Tyne and Wear Metro 45

1981

Rail Policy 50
Barmouth Bridge 52
Review of Main Line Electrification 54
DMU Replacement 56
Winter Weather and the APT debut 58

1982

New Sleeping Cars 64
Industrial Strife 66
The Parcels Business 68
Heavy Freight Locomotives 70
West Coast Infrastructure Review 72

1983

The Serpell Report 78
Midland Suburban Electrification 80
The Selby Diversion 82
Government Objectives for British Rail 84
The Docklands Light Railway 86

1984

Rails into Roads 94
Manchester Plans for the Future 96
Gatwick Express 99
Rural Railways review 101
APTIS and Friends 104

1985

InterCity – Into Profit 112
London Regional Transport 116
Electrification Progress 118
Corporate Plan 121

Appendices

British Rail traffic statistics 1978-1985 126
British Rail assets, 1978-1985 127
British Rail business performance indicators, 1980-1985 128

Preface

A diary of events suggests a meticulous day to day account. In a business the size of British Rail, any recording can at best be selective, and in this volume I have therefore attempted to highlight just a few of what appear to have been the major events and achievements in the years under review. All sections of the railway business receive a mention, not forgetting the non-BR services operated in London, Glasgow and Tyne & Wear.

Given a longer time perspective, some of my subject choices may seem curious. Already, after only two years, memory of the name of Serpell has dimmed, while the new generation of ticket machines has yet to achieve all that is claimed for it. But hindsight cannot be exercised currently, and the present compilation is deliberately sparing in the conclusions which it draws.

My primary sources for the written material were the monthly Ian Allan magazine *Modern Railways*, and those important documents, the Railways Board's *Annual Reports and Accounts*. I have also enjoyed generous help with photographs from my colleagues in the Phoenix Railway Photographic Circle, whose work enhances these pages. With the long drawn out timescale of many railway events, judgements have had to be made as to the year in which they and the photographs should be included. I have tried to avoid anachronisms, but I trust that the reader will forgive any which he spots.

John Glover
Ewell, Surrey

1978

'A year of success and strain' – Sir Peter Parker

Above right:
The Inverness-Kyle of Lochalsh line is 'a rare quintessence of beauty, romance, history, endurance and . . . legend' says the descriptive pamphlet describing the 82¼-mile journey. Never distinguished by the volume of traffic passing over it, British Rail did their best to exploit the line as a tourist attraction.

Right:
The St Erth-St Ives branch in Cornwall found a new raison d'etre in 1978. Jointly financed by the local authorities and BR, a new station was constructed at Lelant Saltings together with a 300 vehicle car park. The scheme was introduced to alleviate chronic traffic congestion in St Ives. The parking fee (initially 60p) included all-day parking and travel by train to either Carbis Bay or St Ives for all the car passengers. Train frequency was doubled to two per hour. In the early season, a Class 118 DMU calls at Carbis Bay on a service to St Erth.
John Glover

Sir Peter Parker's Railway

Peter Parker, Chairman of the Railways Board, had a knighthood conferred on him in the Queen's Birthday Honours in 1978. By then two years into an appointment which was to last for a further five, Parker had had time to assess the industry which he headed. Already, he had formed a strong attachment to devising management targets more workable than pure finance, which could embrace the wider social obligations of running a railway but at the same time still be sufficiently precise to avoid confusion. Above all, objectives needed to be established by which the railways could be operated and against which they could be judged by the community. But what, *Modern Railways* asked him, will the Chairman of BR in 1988 look back over the decade you initiated and be thankful for? In reply, Parker offered a 10-point list of his hopes for achievement:

- A major sustained improvement in relationships between Government and BR leading to the establishment of a positive and stable bi-partisan policy for railways.
- Reinforcement of the watershed conviction contained both in the Government's White Paper and the Report of the Select Committee that railways have a vital and growing contribution to make to the solution of the country's transport problems.
- The development of Board/trade union relationships which will permit us, in partnership, to secure and enlarge the future position of the railway industry.
- Continued improvement in productivity giving value for money for the customer and commensurate rewards for the operators.

Below:
Main line electrification continued to be represented by the sole example of the West Coast main line. The joint Department of Transport/BR working party to review the case was set up, and for a while the outlook appeared promising. Internationally, BR came 17th when judged by the proportion electrified at 2,431 route miles or 21% of the network. This, however, carried 40% of the total train mileage. No 87.002 with a mixture of Mk 1, Mk 2 and Mk 3 stock heads south through the Lune Gorge with a Glasgow-Euston express. The practice of naming locomotives was revived, and No 87.002 was allocated *Royal Sovereign.*
Les Nixon

- The successful and profitable introduction of HST and APT services.
- A significant start on a rolling programme of mainline electrification.
- Sustained and significant improvement in the profitability of the Board's other businesses – the groups within the group.
- The concept of the commonwealth of transport more imaginatively accepted, with more inter-modal experiments and successes.
- The establishment of transport as a whole as central to prosperity and to the industrial strategy; and with it the building up of a common data bank of information to which all can have access.
- Above all, a clean, attractive, well-loaded railway, understandable and understood. One which we can be proud of and which everyone can use and enjoy.

Left:
Parker's paramount priority in day to day terms was to satisfy the customer, and there were fears that the infamous 'crumbling edge of quality' would increasingly inhibit the railways' ability to satisfy. Investment in new rolling stock was extremely limited; other than HST/APT trailers, only 42 new passenger vehicles were built in 1978, and these were all EMUs. Passengers flock to join a new Class 507 unit at Sandhills, en route for the seaside delights of Southport. *John Glover*

Below left:
Much railway work is out of doors; it takes place 24 hours a day, and (nowadays) 363 days a year. The labour force is often supervised only indirectly due to the nature of the industry; there are no confines of factory walls. Self discipline in Parker's 'Community of the Railway' is essential. In this picture the points are cleared of snow at Abergele and Pensarn as the 09.22 Bangor-Manchester Victoria headed by No 47.435 pulls away after making a special stop to counter service disruption caused by the weather.
Larry Goddard

The Return of Freightliners

Freightliners was launched in 1965 following earlier container experiments, and after being given Dr Beeching's approval in his 1963 Reshaping report. The concept was of an inland transportation exercise, a trunk conveyor belt between road-rail transfer centres in the country's principal production areas. But after only three years, Freightliners was placed under the control of the National Freight Corporation which, it was said, would make for an integrated freight sales package. Ten years later, the loss making company had been transformed into a profitable concern, and was returned to British Rail as a subsidiary company on 4 August 1978. Curiously, marketing seems to have been the principal reasoning behind the re-entry into full railway ownership; a keystone of the British Rail case was that full container-on-rail potential needed highly developed and rail-oriented marketing which could not be provided by the relatively small Freightliner company, and that the alternative of two separate marketing operations selling freight by rail was needlessly extravagant.

Whilst the original Freightliner concept had proved sound, optimism had led to an underestimation of the terminal and haulage costs, both for the trunk movements by rail and for the road collection and delivery. Consequently, instead of being competitive

Right:
In 1978 the normal Freightliner train grossed 1,070 tonnes. The first 25 car train was operated on the Nottingham-Glasgow service, but the weight of the container contents was restricted. The aim was 1,500 tonnes gross. Use of Class 56 locomotives increased the horsepower available, and here 4S81 19.45 Pengam-Glasgow passes Llanrumney behind No 56.058.
Michael Rhodes

over 90 miles as forecast by Beeching, 200 miles turned out to be nearer the mark. In the intervening years the motorway network expanded, and the whole pattern of industrial production changed. Freightliners looked elsewhere for their traffic, and whilst lack of enthusiasm by European railway administrations and Irish troubles limited potential in these sectors, deep sea growth was remarkable. By 1978, Freightliners led the field, moving 42% of all inland deep sea containers in the UK. Market share of the export-import business varied, but a high of 60% of Far East traffic was recorded. Indeed, deep sea traffic accounted for 35% of all container capacity moved, compared with 40% for the inland home trade, the remainder being on the short sea routes and Irish traffic.

At home, great store was being set upon the concept of Freightliner Relay, designed to provide a complete production line to the consumer, eliminating the expense of an intermediate warehousing stage and the cost of keeping buffer stocks. The mix of commodities changed. In 1978 food and drink amounted to 27% of home business, followed by parcels (16%), and metals (11%). Subcontracting for hauliers, once regarded as the likely prime users of Freightliners, accounted for only 7% of the total. Trains of 25 wagons in length were tried for the first time (on the Nottingham-Glasgow Coatbridge service) and route availability was being sought for the new 8ft 6in high containers. The original container fleet was by now in need of renewal, together with cranes and road vehicles; however, 65% of containers moved were privately owned. The NFC was sorry to lose the largest overland container haulage operation in the world. 'I regard Sir Peter Parker as jolly lucky', said Sir Daniel Pettitt, the then NFC Chairman.

Left:
Class 31 No 31.157 departs from Nottingham Beeston with a train to Birmingham Lawley Street. On the left, a single Freightliner flat shows its skeletal construction and the fixed bar coupling without conventional drawgear. Wagons are usually run in fixed formation sets of five.
Paul D. Shannon

Below left:
Maritime Freightliner traffic was buoyant. With a depot ideally situated and transfer costs to and from ship negligible, Southampton-London was a viable operation despite the distance of only 80 miles. No 47.060 hurries through Eastleigh with a train for Glasgow Coatbridge. The destination will be reached in under 10 hours.
John Glover

Merseyrail Complete

The first stage of the development of Merseyside's rail system was completed in 1978 with the opening of the former Cheshire Lines Committee route to Garston on 3 January, and the finishing of the Moorfields interchange between the Northern and Wirral lines in July.

The plans for Merseyside dated back to the early 1960s, when the cost of providing a new road system was ruled out and a public transport solution sought instead. British Rail's proposals envisaged extension of the Mersey/Wirral lines under the city centre (the loop), and the southerly extension of the Southport/Ormskirk lines underground via Exchange and Central stations (the link). The effect would be to knit together a number of unrelated radial routes to form a basic integrated rapid transit system with much improved interchange facilities.

The loop is a one-direction single line tunnel 15ft 5in in diameter, diverging from the Mersey Railway's original route below the eastern bank of the river, through a new platform at James Street, to a new station at Moorfields and the deepest point at 124ft below

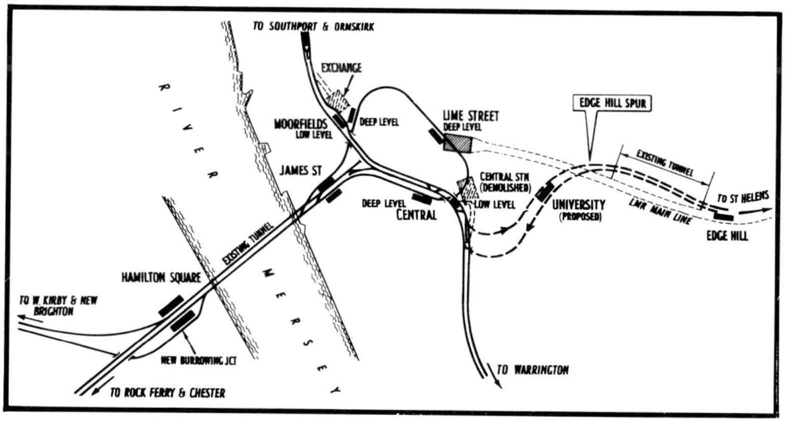

Right:
In 1939 the London Midland & Scottish Railway introduced a series of three-car trains for the Ormskirk and Southport services. Known later as Class 502, these veterans also operated to Garston and Kirkby when the suburban electrification was extended. MBS No M28351M is at the rear of a six-car formation disappearing into the rain on the single track stub from Fazakerley towards the Kirkby terminus.
John Glover

Hatton Garden, through a new underground station at Lime Street and back to the original route just short of James Street station. A burrowing junction and a third platform face were constructed at Hamilton Square to eliminate delays at the flat crossing where the Rock Ferry line diverges from that to West Kirby and New Brighton.

To achieve the north-south link, the lines from Southport/ Ormskirk were diverted north of the Exchange terminal station into a new double track tunnel, through Moorfields and onto the section of the Mersey Railway released by the construction of the loop and Central station. The line then extends south and into the old high level station tunnel and on to Garston. To avoid disruption to services in the future, and to cater for a proposed extension to St Helens, junctions have been formed at the south end of Central station.

Third rail electrification saw the branch to Kirkby on the Wigan line brought into the network, as well as the previously closed branch to Garston. Subsequent extensions were the two miles from Garston to Hunts Cross opened in 1983, and the five miles from Rock Ferry to Hooton in 1985. Further schemes remained under consideration. Deliveries of new Class 507 rolling stock to replace the aged Class 502 LMS units started in 1978, and 43 similar Class 508 units from the Southern Region were transferred to gradually take the place of the Class 503 Wirral line units. Trains are maintained at Birkenhead North and the new depot at Hall Road.

Above left:
The Class 503 units were built in two batches in 1938 and 1956. Of more restricted profile, these units were used on Wirral services and a set of 1956 stock was photographed whilst being stabled for the night in West Kirby sidings at the close of the evening peak. Extensive alteration to allow the provision of end doors was necessary to allow the trains to be used in safety in the single track tunnels constructed as part of the central Liverpool 'Loop'.
John Glover

Left:
The second of the new trains delivered in 1978 calls at Hightown on the Southport line. Despite long established electrification for traction purposes, semaphore signalling is still commonplace on this intensively used commuter railway. The 15 minute all day frequency increased to five minute intervals at the height of the peak.
John Glover

Level Crossing Protection

In the 1950s it was clear that the employment of staff on purely gatekeeping duties at level crossings was becoming more difficult and costly, and there was also a need to reduce delays to road traffic. These arose principally from the time cycle of opening swing gates, which needed to be completed in sufficient time to avoid delaying a train through adverse signals. Lifting barriers first made an appearance in 1954, followed by automatic barriers three years later.

Ever since the Hixon accident of 1968 when an express hit a low loader on an automatic crossing, level crossing modernisation had been painfully slow. Costly extra safety precautions had been imposed on automatic half barrier crossings to the extent that any economies were virtually destroyed, and design simplifications were urgently needed. A working party was established and reported in 1978; six criteria were offered for level crossing design and operation:

- Clear and timely warning to road users of their approach to a level crossing.
- Adequate warning that the road over the crossing is about to be closed or is already closed to road traffic.
- Road traffic should not block automatic level crossings.
- Road characteristics over an automatic crossing should not provide risk of accident.
- Time cycle of automatic crossings should not be so short that long vehicles travelling slowly could not clear the crossing before a train arrived, nor so long that road users would become impatient and disobey road signals.

Below:
If a resident crossing keeper is not provided, it falls to the train crew to open and close the level crossing gates. On the former Caledonian Railway main line between Perth and Aberdeen, the infrequent freight from Perth to Forfar stops at Eassie to allow the second man to perform this necessary ritual. The train locomotive is Class 27 No 27.105. This line is now closed completely.
Cyril Lofthus

Above left:
Two cars dutifully wait at the automatic half-barrier crossing at Silverdale for Class 40 No 40.057 to proceed with the 20.06 Corkickle-Folly Lane train of ICI sodium carbonate tanks. None of the constraints associated with poor visibility or traffic tailbacks are likely to cause problems at country locations such as this. *Kim Fullbrook*

Left:
Manually controlled lifting barriers are installed at Farnham, illuminated by high-intensity lighting. At present the crossing is controlled from the signalbox at the far end of the station, but the installation of CCTV cameras would enable remote control to be instituted with the minimum of further modification. There were 498 such crossings on BR at the beginning of 1978, of which 97 were equipped with CCTV. Class 423 (4VEP) unit No 7853 leaves with an Alton-Waterloo train.
John Glover

- The use of reliable systems but with positive ways of minimising accident risks in the event of equipment failure.

The physical factors to be taken into account included the number and speeds of trains using the crossing, the number of tracks to be crossed, volume and speed of road traffic, and the nature of the locality. Study of European practice had demonstrated that automatic barriers installed there were no less safe in spite of far less stringent requirements, and a number of detailed alterations were recommended as a result. Open, ie ungated, crossings of various types were also considered, and it was thought that much wider use could be made of these on roads carrying up to 200 vehicles a day if train speeds were limited to 10mph.

The report recommended a 10 year modernisation programme to convert about 1,000 manned crossings to automatic operation, with about 360 automatic open crossings, 470 automatic half barriers, and 200 manually controlled barriers supervised by closed circuit television.

GN Suburban Electrification

The Great Northern suburban electrification scheme, thought by many to be at least a quarter of a century overdue, was formally opened on 13 March. The shabby diesel-hauled and DMU operated suburban services were replaced by new electric units with enhanced service levels and faster timings. Whilst the inner suburban services from Hertford North and Welwyn Garden City ran to Moorgate over the tracks of the former Northern City line of London Transport, the newly inaugurated outer suburban services operated from the spruced up and rationalised King's Cross.

The initial service, maintained by Class 312/0 units built by British Rail Engineering Ltd at York, operated half-hourly, calling at Finsbury Park, Potters Bar, Hatfield and all stations to Royston in an overall timing of 62 minutes for the 45 miles. On top of this pattern, an hourly fast service was imposed, with calls at Stevenage, Hitchin and Letchworth only. In the peak hour, seven departures from King's Cross were provided between 17.00 and 17.59, which required careful timing so as not to disrupt the InterCity services on the 2½-mile two-track section between Welwyn and Woolmer Green, and also at the flat junction for the Cambridge branch at Hitchin. Approaching King's Cross, the realigned Holloway flyover ensured the effective separation of the suburban trains. Although electrified, initial services north of Hertford on the loop were provided exclusively by an irregular hourly DMU service running to Huntingdon, connecting at Stevenage out of the fast Royston trains. DMUs also provided the hourly service from Royston to Cambridge, off-peak trains running alternately all stations and non-stop.

Electrification caused a real growth in travel as opposed to diversions from other forms of transport, particularly in the peak. In the outer suburban area this occurred mostly at stations serving

Below:
For the GN outer-suburban electrification, 26 four-car units were built of Class 312/0; they were generally similar to the Class 310 units supplied to the London Midland Region in 1966, and were themselves supplemented by trains for the GE line and LMR Birmingham area services. Unit No 312.711 was photographed in Hornsey depot, where all the GN line EMU stock is maintained. *John Glover*

Below right:
The open countryside beyond Baldock would not in itself justify electrification. Class 312/0 No 312.713 was photographed near Litlington crossing on the four mile stretch between Royston and Ashwell & Morden as it worked the 11.38 local service to King's Cross. *John C. Baker*

the large towns of Stevenage, Hitchin, Letchworth and Royston, where overall journey times to central London were greatly improved, but from which relatively few people commute to London anyway. In these towns residential development was still underway, and there was an underlying growth in commuting. Electrification also proved advantageous in much enhancing the effectiveness of the service, and improved a public transport asset. It thus offered benefits to the community well beyond those of immediate traffic gains.

Above:
Permission was refused to extend electrification to Cambridge. A Class 101 diesel multiple-unit leaves Foxton for Royston, where it will connect into a fast London service. In 1978 the scheduled journey time from Cambridge to King's Cross inclusive of the change and three intermediate stops was 73 minutes, compared with 63 minutes for the two-mile shorter non-stop run to Liverpool Street. *John Glover*

1978

Left:
The last semaphore signals on the ECML were at Doncaster, and were taken out of service with due ceremony in autumn 1978. Multiple-aspect signalling then extended throughout to Edinburgh, although north of York there were many small signalboxes with limited control areas. A BRCW DMU approaches Black Carr Junction with a Lincoln-Doncaster service.
Les Nixon

Right:
In May 1978 the East Coast main line became the second BR trunk route to introduce 125mile/h HST workings. These were confidently expected to produce a far greater impact on the passenger business than that achieved on the Western Region. The 'Flying Scotsman' now reached Newcastle in 3hr 4min, and Edinburgh in 4hr 52min. For the time being, limitations were imposed by the late delivery of stock, and the train plan was complicated by the retention of numerous 100mph services. No 254.009 was photographed passing Wood Green with a down express. *John Glover*

Below right:
The London Brick Company renewed their contract for carriage of containerised bricks from Stewartby, Bedfordshire to London and to Liverpool/Manchester. The bricks are conveyed in open topped containers, each of which has a 6,700 brick capacity. Incoming rail traffic consists of containerised domestic refuse from various London Boroughs and is used as fill to reclaim worked out clay pits. The 13.21 'Fletliner' to Garston is seen between Bedford St Johns and Midland stations behind Nos 25.266 and 25.315. The brick traffic ceased in 1984.
Paul D. Shannon

Left:
In the first five days of the Motor Show, staged for the first time at the National Exhibition Centre, Birmingham, 161,000 persons passed through Birmingham International. Train services from New Street were substantially augmented with an EMU shuttle running every 10 minutes, and up to five special trains an hour were provided from Euston in addition to the basic half-hourly service. The latter proved over generous, while business from the north was underestimated. No 86.247 pauses at International with the 11.29 Wolverhampton-Euston on 21 October.
Chris Davis

Below left:
In May, local passenger services were restored to the Longbridge-Birmingham New Street line, and proved an instant success. Four services an hour were increased to six during the peaks, and 34 three-car DMUs were required to operate the service which runs through to Four Oaks on the Lichfield line. Two new stations were built, and others refurbished. Five Ways, seen here, originally closed in 1944 and was reopened to serve offices and a residential area. A Class 116 DMU emerges from Bath Row tunnel, the last of five between here and New Street. *John Glover*

Right:
The 1970s were the years of coordination and integration, and interchange between transport modes was acknowledged as a sensible part of an overall planned public transport system. Altrincham Interchange represented one of the best examples of its type, with the local bus services wholly dovetailed into the rail services. A Class 304/1 EMU lurks in the station whilst in the foreground is a Bristol coach of the National Bus Company's Crosville subsidiary and a Greater Manchester PTE Leyland National. *John Glover*

Below right:
'In evaluating the role of public transport in rural areas, I must say this: rail wants to sustain its vital contribution to rural services, but the cost of that contribution is growing. There are many options, including the integration of bus and rail services, but these options must be exposed and some decisions faced before choice is overtaken by economic necessity.' – Sir Peter Parker. A Liskeard-Looe train maintained by a single Class 121 DMU arrives at Coombe Junction for reversal. All signalling has since been removed and the track layout simplified. *John Glover*

1979

'A year of harsh success' – Sir Peter Parker

Above right:
In the initial Family Railcard scheme, the first adult paid the ordinary fare, with others paying 50p only. Interestingly, the passenger was still supposed to recognise the traditional Edmondson card ticket in preference to the many mechanised issues.

Right:
A new build of 43 trains for the South Western inner-suburban services from Waterloo commenced delivery from the York works of BREL. No 508.013 leads a peak hour Shepperton via Richmond service out of Waterloo. Five years later these trains were transferred to Merseyside, minus one of the trailers, which was retained to be included in the replacement Class 455 units. *John Glover*

European Rail Performance

Comparative studies of the performance of the railway business with that of the main Continental railway administrations were completed in 1979. The aims were to identify differences and to establish the extent to which they were the consequence of geography and economic structure, of government policy on the role of railways and competition, or resulted from the internal characteristics of management and operation of the railways themselves. Thus British Rail would be helped to identify those areas in which its own performance was least satisfactory.

With such a wide ranging study, it was perhaps open inevitably to the charge that statistics can be made to prove what one wants them to prove. On government involvement, for instance, the only general conclusion to be drawn was that no two railway systems were treated alike, although it was acknowledged that government attitudes and policies were a major influence, whether in the commercial, operating or financial performance fields.

British Rail had no doubts as to the most important messages. There was shown to be a strong correlation between the extent to which the costs of running the railway were covered by the customers rather than through government support, the general level of fares charged, and the market share of the railway undertaking. Thus while both British Rail and Swedish Railways (SJ) were covering over 70% of their costs, Italian Railways (FS) covered only 32%. At the same time fare levels on BR and SJ were twice those of FS, while FS had twice the market share at around 12% of the total passenger kilometres by all means of transport, compared with BR (6½%) and SJ (5½%). It was concluded that government policies on support levels were the main determinant of fares levels, and that fares in turn provided the major explanation of different levels of use of the passenger railway.

Investment level comparisons were complicated by the different methods of calculation, but however this was carried out BR was

Below:
The perception of the railway as it would wish to be seen: an IC125 unit with the morning up 'Leeds Executive' hurries towards King's Cross as a Class 313 inner suburban EMU retires to Hornsey depot at the end of the morning peak.
John Glover

shown as receiving very little compared with FS and Belgian Railways (SNCB), both of which came out consistently high.

Labour productivity was of considerable interest, and the hours worked per member of staff on BR were found to be 30% above the other eight European railways. However, these long hours did not result in higher levels of output per man; it was thought that six day standard working weeks rather than seven as used on the Continent, and the lack of flexibility in BR rostering practices were contributory factors. Thus whilst output per employee in terms of train kilometres operated was relatively good, the average British railwayman had to work far longer hours than his counterpart, and was less well paid too. For train crew, BR did rather well for passenger trains, together with SJ, NS (Dutch Railways) and SNCF (French Railways). But in the freight and parcels sector the BR and FS performance was much worse than any other railway, requiring more than twice as many crew as the more efficient railways. The overwhelming cause was that other systems had largely abolished guards and/or drivers' assistants on freight trains. The potential revealed here for increased productivity was thought to be the clearest conclusion to emerge from the entire study.

Above left:
The decision to equip diesel-electric locomotives with boilers to enable them to supply steam for carriage heating purposes appears curious today, although the alternative cost of converting up to 30,000 passenger coaches to electric heating weighed heavily at the time. With a 1978 total fleet of 6,000 coaches the problem was becoming manageable, and steam heating was being phased out. Few other railway administrations would have taken so long to rid themselves of such an inherently unsatisfactory system. Class 40 No 40.033 shows it has copious amounts of steam available to heat the 07.55 to Inverness, seen here before departure from Aberdeen. *Kim Fullbrook*

Left:
Class 47 No 47.474 receives a quick window cleaning at the Ranelagh Road stabling point outside Paddington; note the effort-reducing use made of the locomotive's lamp bracket! Labour accounts for nearly 60% of rail operating costs, and the productive use of labour thus becomes the key to financial performance. *Les Nixon*

Passenger Marketing

The year saw a major offensive on the passenger marketing front. The name of the game was maximising passenger journeys and, it was hoped, revenue. Of all the modes of transport, rail was the best suited to carry large numbers of passengers and, what was more, the capacity was mostly available to do it. Even if no extra revenue were to be generated, BR could justifiably claim that the taxpayer's contribution was being better spent; more journeys would be made for the same call on public funds.

Whilst the business market was not felt to be unduly price sensitive, sales efforts were to be redoubled with, for the first time, a series of mail shots. It was the leisure market where competition was at its height, and ignorance of the availability of cheap fares was seen as a prime target.

Although rail travel for the individual is not particularly costly, it quickly becomes uncompetitive when a family group travels together. If, as is often the case, there is a car available for the journey, sheer economics dictate its use. Such thinking presaged the launch of the Family Railcard which in its original form allowed one member of the family to travel at the ordinary (full) or day return fare, and a second adult and up to four children to travel at a flat fare of 50p each.

1979 was also the International Year of the Child, and two further innovations were the raising of the lower age limit at which child fares became payable from three to five years, and the formation of the Great Rail Club. With its title later changed to Rail Riders (the happiest club in the land) and a Class 47 locomotive carrying the name also, members receive books of discount vouchers for reduced rate rail travel and a regular magazine.

Below:
In commercial terms, HST operation was an outstanding success. Volume growth was three times the InterCity average, and the 1979 sales campaign was to feature HST prominently. Passengers throng the platform at Paddington after a punctual arrival from South Wales.
John Glover

Far left:
The Great Rail Club was established in 1979 to attract the younger generation to rail travel.

Left:
The Family Railcard was added to the Senior Citizen and Student Railcards already available. A Class 108 DMU pauses at Elsecar with a Leeds-Sheffield via Barnsley service, and picks up a number of young people. Because of its pricing structure, the Family Railcard is of little value on short journeys, and its use on busy pay-trains is complex to say the least! *Les Nixon*

Below:
Trans-Pennine services were the subject of special promotion following their reshaping with the introduction of additional locomotive hauled trains and early Mk 2 rolling stock. No 47.408 leaves Stalybridge with the 13.05 Liverpool Lime Street-York, passing the 11.56 Hull-Manchester Victoria formed of one of the Class 124 DMUs built for the route and which were being displaced. *Larry Goddard*

Scottish Achievements

The collapse of Penmanshiel tunnel on 17 March blocked the northern end of the East Coast main line (ECML) between Berwick and Dunbar for an extended period, and services could only be restored via a new diversion on 20 August. Whilst emergency timetables allowed for local services to be provided by buses, ECML trains to be diverted via Carlisle, and additional services run between Aberdeen/Edinburgh and Euston, all thoughts of implementing the accelerated HST timetable in May had to be scrapped.

Commercially, the tunnel collapse could not have come at a worse time. By mid-March, the first year of partial HST working was nearing completion, and a major marketing effort was under way. Objectives had to be switched to minimise delays and inconvenience, and 4hr 37min timings between London and Edinburgh had to wait.

A major innovation which did take place was the complete revamp of the Edinburgh-Glasgow service. Because of the nature of the route, with a high ratio of turnround time to journey time, it was decided to retain the push-pull concept, but using more powerful locomotives and modern stock. Air-conditioning, more seats and improved reliability were seen as essential, and the eventual choice fell upon the use of Class 47/7 locomotives (modified for push-pull operation), Mk 3 coaches and a Mk 2f Brake Second converted to a Driving Trailer (DBSO). The new six-coach trains provided a half-hourly service. The existing lighting circuits were used to transmit the control signals from the DBSO to the locomotive, which is always at the Edinburgh end of the train.

Below:
Before the collapse: 'Deltic' No 55.021 *Argyll and Sutherland Highlanders* is about to plunge into Penmanshiel Tunnel with the 12.12 Edinburgh Waverley-King's Cross. The work in the tunnel was intended to provide clearance for 8ft 6in high containers, then coming into increasing use on Freightliner services. *Cyril Lofthus*

Below right:
Through journey times between London and Edinburgh via Carlisle for the three retained East Coast trains were about 5hr 35min, and the availability of IC125 sets eased the reversal at Carstairs. On 7 July, an HST is repositioned at Carstairs prior to returning to Edinburgh; this set was being used for a shuttle service to Edinburgh and Dunbar. *Cyril Lofthus*

Left:
Bridgeton station on the Argyle line replaced the previous Bridgeton in what is now a carriage depot only. The reopened station is situated in a cutting between two tunnels; No 314.213 is seen arriving with a service for Dalmuir via Yoker. Of note is the display of the station name on the walls and also the use of slab track, found on much of the new link. *John Glover*

October saw the inauguration of the Argyle line in Glasgow linking the hitherto separate systems north and south of the Clyde, the most significant rail development in the area since the original electrification of the 1960s. The project centred on the reopening of the former Glasgow Central Low Level line from Kelvinhaugh Junction near Partick to Rutherglen on the West Coast main line (WCML). New stations were provided at Rutherglen (replacing the existing), Dalmarnock, Bridgeton (replacing the existing), Argyle Street, Central Low Level, Anderston, Finnieston and Partick (replacing Partick Hill), which was provided with direct interchange to the Underground. Much improving access to central Glasgow, the new link offered an opportunity to restructure services and improve rolling stock utilisation. A series of 16 Class 314 electric units was constructed to operate the augmented services.

Below:
A DBSO leads a push-pull train from Edinburgh into Glasgow Queen Street. These trains took over from the early Mk 2 sets with a Class 27 locomotive at each end which had operated the service since 1971, but which were felt to be commercially less than adequate besides having an unacceptably high failure rate in service.
John Glover

Centenary of Train Catering

1979 was celebrated as the Centenary of Train Catering in Britain. A special train formed of historic restaurant, buffet and Pullman cars, together with a Mk 1 vehicle to undertake the actual cooking, toured provincial centres in the autumn. The itinerary culminated in a run from Leeds to King's Cross on 13 September. On its arrival, Sir Peter Parker took the opportunity to spell out British Rail's plans for new and refurbished catering vehicles over the next four years.

Whilst £9million was to be allocated to HST catering cars and £4million to APT vehicles, most interest centred around the £4million set aside for refurbishment and the micro-buffet concept. The idea was to provide a basic catering service on trains where more elaborate facilities were not justified. Initial conversions were being carried out on Mk 1 Brake Second Open coaches. The work involved removing two seating bays adjacent to the toilet compartment, from which the pedestal was removed but the wash basin and plumbing retained. A fully laden trolley containing

Below:
Birmingham-Norwich trains were selected as being the first to benefit from the introduction of Micro-Buffets, a journey of all but four hours on even the fastest of the services offered. An unidentified Class 31 stands in Leicester on 21 September with the 08.05 from Birmingham New Street, one of the trains with no refreshment facilities at all. On the left the new station buildings are nearly complete; work has yet to start on the demolition of the down side.
John Glover

everything necessary to provide a snack service would be taken on board and slotted into the modified area where it would become part of the counter. Early trials were on the Birmingham-Norwich services.

In view of the continued use of Mk 1 catering cars on many routes, about 200 vehicles were to be refurbished with modern decor, new tables and counters, and refrigerators. These were being supplemented by a series of 28 locomotive-hauled Mk 3 buffet restaurant cars with unclassified seating for the London Midland Region electrified services.

After its periodic return to the doldrums, train catering in 1979 was said to be regarded 'very firmly' as part of the total travel concept and as a loss leader to be guaranteed under a marketing approach to passenger services. Breakfast accounted for nearly half the total set train meals served, and was recognised as being an integral part of the business travel package. A long term contract was being negotiated with Travellers Fare under which the passenger business would lay down the level of catering for each individual service, Travellers Fare would establish the cost of providing it, and BR would agree the amount and the conditions under which the catering loss should be subsidised from rail fares. Traditional full meals were to continue on main line InterCity routes, but on all Southern Region services buffet or griddle type catering was deemed to be sufficient.

Above:
No 47.543 heads the up 'Centenary Express' as it approaches Finsbury Park on 13 September. The vehicles were provided by the National Railway Museum at York. Other venues visited were Southampton, Cardiff, Bristol, Birmingham, Manchester, Edinburgh and Newcastle.
Martin Higginson

EMU Refurbishing

During 1979 the programme of refurbishing Southern Region EMU stock was begun by BREL at their Swindon workshops. First trains to be dealt with were the 'CEP' express stock built for the Kent Coast electrification from 1956 onwards; the Southern, with the largest EMU fleet on British Rail, was expected to provide eventually well over 60% of the cars to be refurbished.

Ideally, elderly rolling stock is replaced with a new build, but investment restrictions and the fact that (at 1979 prices) a new four car set would cost £600,000 compared with £250,000 for an updating tipped the scales in favour of the latter. This would extend the life of each set by up to 20 years, and at the same time reduce maintenance costs. Improvements in ventilation, new second class seating in open saloons rather than compartments, and new decor were all intended to increase the appeal to the customer.

Few of the materials removed from the original sets were reused, and only the underframes, bodyshell, external doors and motor bogies remained as in the original version. Internal layout revisions

Below right:
1956 stock prototypes were also included in the programme, and parts of unit No 7101 are seen inside the works. All second class seating was converted to open accommodation, barring one compartment which was retained. First class seats remained in compartments. Seating capacities overall hardly varied for the four car units, with second class reduced from 200 to 198 and first class constant at 24.
Michael J. Collins

Below:
A pair of Class 411/2 Driving Motor Brake Seconds from Kent Coast units Nos 7156 and 7211 stand outside Swindon Works. They have already been gutted, with the brake compartment behind the driving cabs removed in the course of their conversion for use as passenger accommodation.
John Glover

removed the brake van accommodation provided in each of the driving motor cars, and replaced them with a single luggage/guards compartment in an intermediate trailer.

Work was broken down into 10 stages, starting with stripping down. Blue asbestos removal formed the next part of the work in controlled conditions. Corroded areas were cut away and replaced, and pillars repositioned to take account of the new internal layout. Vehicle lifting was the opportunity to replace bogies with the Commonwealth design recovered from condemned locomotive-hauled stock. New woodwork, pipework and electrical wiring were then installed, together with the plumbing. Public address was fitted, doors hung, and double glazed windows installed. Surface finishing then allowed Mk 3 style seats and the floor coverings to be fitted. Finishing touches included new toilet units and the provision of heaters, followed by extensive testing.

Similar work has since been carried out elsewhere, notably on London area units of the Eastern Region. A prime requirement there was to provide gangway connections throughout each unit as part of the refurbishing process. Major DMU classes have also been treated.

Below:
Back in their traditional haunts, No 411.513 at the head of a 12-car formation speeds through Kent having just emerged from the 1m 851yd Polhill tunnel between Knockholt and Dunton Green. Despite the much improved internal appearance, passengers were incensed by the discomfort of the new seats which, it was admitted, were less comfortable than they should have been.
Colin J. Marsden

1979

Right:
Services in both the Liverpool Street and South Eastern Divisions were disrupted by a shortage of guards, leading to many train cancellations. Despite recruitment and training of 370 new guards the position had not improved by the end of the year. The service was running like clockwork at Wickford with Class 302 unit No 207 arriving with a Liverpool Street-Southend Victoria train and the Southminster branch service consisting of a Cravens Class 105 DMU waiting in the up side bay. *John Glover*

Right:
London Transport commenced public services on the 2¾ miles of the Jubilee Line from Baker Street to Charing Cross on 1 May, following formal opening by HRH Prince Charles on 30 April. The line took over the Stanmore branch of the Bakerloo, and provides in-town relief to that line. It was intended to project the line through the City to Fenchurch Street and beyond, but the project has since been abandoned. A 1972 Mk 2 stock train arrives at the southbound platform at Baker Street.
John Glover

Right:
Track simplification is a useful means of cost-cutting, and the Ashford-Hastings line was singled during the year. A passing loop was retained at Rye. Seen leaving Ore on the singled line is Class 206 No 1206; the track on the left is now merely a headshunt for electric trains to gain access to their depot. The lack of a third rail on the other track will be noted.
John Glover

Left:
In North Wales, the Conwy Valley line from Llandudno Junction up to Blaenau Ffestiniog celebrated its centenary. Summer Sunday services were again restored to the line courtesy Gwynedd County Council, under charter from BR. Amid the huge piles of slate, the 09.37 to Llandudno approaches the mouth of the 2m 338yd single bore tunnel which leads to the head of the Conwy Valley proper.
John Glover

Below left:
Yet another centenary celebrated was that of world electric traction for rail purposes. In Britain the oldest contender is the Volks Railway at Brighton, but the Manx Electric Railway is perhaps the most venerable antique in these islands. Running the whole year round, all the rolling stock was built between 1893 and 1906 and remains in its original condition. On the 3ft gauge, Winter Saloon No 21 of 1899 and a 'Toastrack' trailer toil up under Ballagorry bridge en route from Ramsey to Douglas.
John Glover

Above:
October 1979 saw the introduction of four HST acelerated services between Paddington, Plymouth and Penzance, with the full timetable following in May 1980. The route was not ideally suited, with 125mph only attainable east of Reading. Nevertheless, the down 'Cornish Riviera' managed 3hr 13min to Plymouth and 5hr 18min to Penzance. Here an up express runs along the sea wall between Parsons and Coryton tunnels at Dawlish. *John Glover*

1980

'A grim, demanding year' – Sir Peter Parker

Above:
Promotions featured both Kelloggs and the products of Lever Bros. This 1980 leaflet was in respect of Persil tickets.

Right:
A parade of motive power took place at Rainhill in May. Before the event, the L&M's *Lion* 0-4-2 of 1838 was restored at the Vulcan Works of Ruston Diesels at Newton-le-Willows. It is seen here undergoing trials at Burscough on 12 May, prior to taking part in the parade two days later. It was subsequently retired to the Merseyside County Museum. *Les Nixon*

London and South-East Commuters

Political dissatisfaction with London and South East commuter services led to a reference to the Monopolies & Mergers Commission. If it was hoped that BR would be exposed as an uncaring, inherently inefficient and badly managed supplier of transport services blatantly exploiting its monopoly position (to quote *Modern Railways*), the report would have come as a profound disappointment. For whilst there were strictures, thus 'We find that to some extent the Board could reduce their costs by improved efficiency without reducing the quality of service they provide', these were of little consequence compared with the MMC's concluding observations:

'The first concerns the commuter's aspirations. Stated in the simplest terms, this is for an adequate service and a punctual train providing a seat in a reasonably clean coach. This is modest enough, but to satisfy it on a railway system as complex and as highly utilised as that in London and its surroundings is not a simple matter. There are direct connections between the level of service which can be provided and the price which is paid for it, and between the frequency of the service and its reliability . . .'

'Our second observation concerns the effect of the financial constraints under which the Board work. On the one hand, they have brought a new awareness at all levels of management of the need to operate the social railway with due regard to economy . . . On the other hand, arbitrary cuts have sometimes been made in response to a particular crisis and on occasion have been subsequently restored . . .'

'Our third observation . . . concerns the future. The problem of the inter-relation of service, costs and charges cannot be tackled

Below:
What the Southern is all about: respectable commuters jockey for seats at Guildford on an up peak train to Waterloo.
John Glover

Below right:
Oldest of the London and South East commuter stock in 1980 were the 4-SUB units of Class 405/2 built to Southern Railway design and dating back to 1948. Unit No 4692 arrives at Clapham Junction with a Horsham-Victoria service on a wet day in the morning peak. An eight-car train of this stock provided seating for approximately 800.
John Glover

satisfactorily unless the business is being conducted with a clear objective. The 1974 direction (referring to the continuing requirement to provide a service broadly comparable to that then offered), however useful it may have been in the past, is no longer adequate for this purpose. We found uncertainty . . . about the limitations which it places on management's discretion . . . It is urgently necessary that the Government should redefine the objective which the Board are to be expected to achieve in operating the social railway . . .'

In response, British Rail produced a new edition of *The Commuters' Charter*, pompously subtitled 'The Foundation of a Progressive Community Served by a Dynamic Railway'. It discussed the old problems of: Who benefits? Who pays? Who should pay? It also listed the benefits which the community could hope to secure from a higher standard of service in the rail system:

- Enhanced opportunities for employment and economic development in Central London and South East England generally.
- Greater prosperity for London's commercial, retail and entertainment facilities.
- Quicker and more comfortable journeys for rail travellers; less road congestion, fewer accidents, and reduced atmospheric pollution for road users and the community at large.
- Significant energy savings.
- A much more cost-effective, high-productivity railway system, where there is a real possibility of containing costs and hence stabilising fares.
- A worthwhile market for British manufacturing industry, where export potential is considerable.

The price tag was put at £1,000million in capital investment over 10 years, which would increase the Public Service Obligation payment requirement by £45million annually by 1990. Some hope!

Below:
The newest stock appeared as Class 315 on the Liverpool Street inner services. No 315.814 passes Bethnal Green on a Gidea Park-Liverpool Street working, while a Class 312 unit disappears towards Colchester. Eight cars of '315' stock provide a mere 632 seats, but with much greater comfort for those who have to stand. *John Glover*

InterCity 1980

By mid-1980, HSTs were operational on the Paddington-Bristol/South Wales routes, and on the ECML. Full West of England services were introduced in May, and in that year the InterCity business as a whole pulled in revenue of £460million. The entry into service of additional HST sets released locomotives and rolling stock for the cascade programme; for example, the East Coast 'Deltics' were to be found for a time on lesser duties such as the Trans-Pennine services across to Manchester and Liverpool before they were finally retired.

In retrospect, the preoccupation with the Advanced Passenger Train seems to have cast a form of planning blight over InterCity developments. For while air-conditioned coaching stock of Mk 2 and, later, Mk 3 varieties was introduced on the important West Coast main line services, the services themselves showed little development from the original electrification timetables. Since the genesis of the APT idea in 1962, the project passed through many vicissitudes, and in the early 1980s it seemed that 'squadron service' was not very far away. Press articles declared APT as central to BR strategy for the rest of the century, and indeed a convincing case was made. Given the worst combination of circumstances, the risk of the APT-S project on the WCML not breaking even on a 7½% rate of return was put officially at three parts in a thousand.

But APT did not appear, and the business had to go on. Neither, for that matter, was there any Government commitment to main line electrification or the Channel Tunnel, both projects dear to the railway heart. Before the onset of the recession, Inter-City was well on the way to achieving its commercially set targets; a contribution of £90million to overheads in 1979 was budgeted to grow by 12% in 1980. By mid-year, costs of locomotive maintenance and fuel were rising, at the same time as revenue particularly from business travel fell away. Action to reduce costs became imperative. Late in 1980 a 5% service reduction was implemented; the coaching stock fleet was purged further of elderly Mk 1 vehicles, and catering services were trimmed. In October, long distance coaches were freed from quantity licencing controls, and began to set about competing systematically with InterCity.

Below:
Cuts of 20min in the Waterloo-Exeter schedules were made possible by the substitution of Laira-based Class 50 power for Southern Class 33s. With long sections of the route west of Salisbury singled, and a multiple stopping pattern on the two-hourly train service, prospects never seemed particularly bright. It was hoped that the service improvement, which included newer stock, would sustain signs of business growth. No 50.011 *Centurion* emerges from Buckhorn Weston tunnel with the 15.20 Exeter-Waterloo.
Michael J. Collins

Below right:
In the twilight of their years, the 'Deltics' still brought a touch of sparkle to the stopping trains between York and King's Cross to which they had been relegated. With an eight-coach formation, as previously used on the Executive services between London and Newcastle, West Yorkshire and Hull, No 55.011 *The Royal Northumberland Fusiliers* passes Helpston with the 10.45 from York.
John C. Baker

Left:
A new feature of the 1980 timetable was the routeing of some services from London to the West Country via the Great Way Round and Bristol. Due to the much faster line speeds permissible on the Bristol route, the journey time penalty was only 15min, whilst the trains could serve as needed reliefs to the services via Newbury. An IC125 leaves Temple Meads for Exeter and Paignton.
John Glover

Centre left:
The vision of APT featured strongly in 1980 planning, with APT-P units currently undergoing an intensive period of pre-service test running and crew training. It was to be 1984 before a highly successful run was made on a much modified unit between Euston and Glasgow in 3hr 52min, and by then it was clear that development plans had moved away from the APT concept. Running as a service train 'relief', and with the black window surrounds applied later, No 370.007 hurries a Glasgow train through Leyland.
Les Nixon

Left:
The Midland line continued as previously; indeed the Midland scene was still a 1950s style railway, albeit with the addition of air-conditioned rolling stock. No clear ideas were emerging about the future, and push-pull operation with Class 47/7s was being talked about as a pre-APT solution. On a fine June evening, a Class 45/1 hauled service approaches Kettering from the south. *John Glover*

Glasgow Underground

Although the Glasgow Underground was formally opened by Her Majesty the Queen late in 1979, public opening was delayed until 16 April 1980. The quaint Glasgow Subway with its original wooden-bodied cars, themselves converted from cable haulage, gave way to a modern Metro system.

The orange livery of the Metro-Cammell built rolling stock gave the system its popular name of the 'Clockwork Orange'. With a 4ft track gauge and restricted tunnel dimensions, vehicle widths are a mere 7ft 8in, 6in less than most buses, which gives a decidedly miniature appearance. Seating in the 33 identical cars is all longitudinal with capacity for 34, plus up to another 56 standing. All trains are formed of two or three cars. One person operation with automatic train operation is the rule, with trackside transponders controlling the trains. The train operator is in charge of the doors, and starts the train by depressing two buttons.

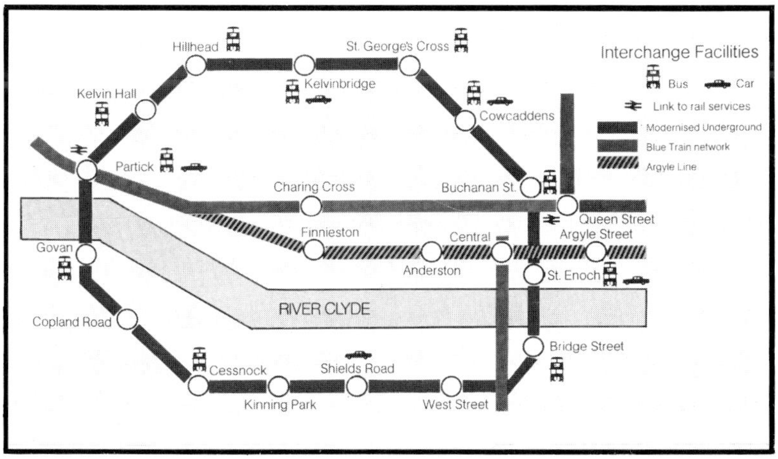

Right:
Map of Glasgow Underground system.

Below:
A two-car train on Strathclyde PTE's Underground arrives at Hillhead. All of the stations were rebuilt before the line reopened in 1980; here the original island platform has been supplemented by a side platform which keeps the two flows of passengers separate. Problems with water seepage into the system are evident on the unoccupied track.
John Glover

The track layout is two concentric circles for inner and outer rail trains, with access to Broomloan depot by ramps from either circuit replacing the car lift formerly in use. Broomloan has a pitted maintenance shed where examinations and inspections are undertaken, as well as areas for full repair and renovation work.

Although there is a flat fare for the system, all 15 stations are staffed. Closed circuit television monitoring is available as is public address at all stations, and drivers are kept in contact by radio. Running time for the 6½mile circuit is 22min, and this is achieved within a maximum permitted speed of 33mph.

When modernisation rather than closure was decided on in 1973, patronage had been falling steadily for years. It was hoped that the declining inner city areas served would be regenerated with the help of the investment. Early forecasts of a complete reversal of the decline proved unduly optimistic, but after a shaky start when an annual rate of 8million passenger journeys per annum was being achieved, patronage increased steadily, and the Strathclyde Passenger Transport Executive was hopeful that revenue would fully cover operating costs in 1984/5, with patronage around 13million.

Below:
Broomloan maintenance shed sees cars undergoing examination. There is a separate lifting shop in which car bodies are removed from their bogies, and also a machine shop which contains a bogie repair area, and a welding shop.
John Glover

Bottom:
One of the original subway cars No 55 in its red livery remained at Broomloan in 1980; another is in the Glasgow Museum of Transport and others are stored at Beamish, County Durham. The cars had doors on one side only, as with island platforms throughout the system, the platform was always on the same side.
John Glover

Wagonload Freight

'The way to break with the past is not to attempt an overall change of the present system but to develop new services, with new rolling stock not compatible with the old, which will progressively displace the common user wagon fleet and the system of operation which employs it'.
From *The Reshaping of British Railways*, 1963

Whilst Beeching may have been popularly associated with the expression 'the basic unit of movement is the train', his views on wagonload traffics were not nearly as dismissive as have been portrayed. In 1980, the development of Speedlink wagonload services was heralded as the rising star of the Railfreight business.

The Speedlink concept is of a limited number of controlled capacity air-braked trunk trains operating overnight between a small number of selected yards. Here, wagons are exchanged between trains which have already been assembled in sections, or they may be collected/distributed by local trip services in the area served by each yard. Fast transits improve service quality and productivity, and the time spent in marshalling and the costs associated with wholesale sorting of trains were all but eliminated. The intention was that each of the dozen or so main yards should have a direct service to each of the others at least once every 24hr.

By 1980, Speedlink was growing fast and making a contribution to overhead costs. In that year the number of trunk services rose from 38 to 58, with an 8% rise in tonnage despite the loss of steel traffic as a consequence of the national steel strike. Part of the growth came from the traditional wagonload network, by then in

Below:
After a stop at Taunton to collect a Taunton Cider Company wagon, No 45.056 rejoins the West of England main line at Taunton East Junction with the 09.05 St Blazey-Severn Tunnel Junction Speedlink freight service. The second wagon contains cement from Chacewater, and the next five are 'Tiger' clay wagons from St Blazey.
Geoff Gillham

Left:
Traditional wagon load traffic required trains to be propelled from marshalling yard reception sidings over the hump, to be sorted in a fan of sidings. At Tees Yard, No 08.085 has just dispatched a cut of four coal hoppers over the hump, to be followed shortly after by the brake van. The special signal provides instructions to the driver of the hump shunter. *Paul D. Shannon*

terminal decline, but the rest was new to rail, in part due to cooperative ventures with other transport operators. As the network of services grew and the trunk flows increased in frequency, so the ability of the system to accept more customers and more varied requirements expanded also. Investment in new wagons had been forthcoming, both for railway owned vehicles and from the private owners. This process was assisted by the Section 8 grants made under the Railways Act 1974, which contributed to the cost of terminal installations and wagons to put traffic on rail 'where it is both economical and environmentally desirable so to do'.

Below:
Marshalling yards are huge consumers of land, which has to be accurately graded as this view of Tinsley, Sheffield, shows. A pair of Class 20 locomotives arrive with a train from the Treeton direction. The vehicle in the centre of the picture is a snowplough. *Les Nixon*

Above:
Class 37 haulage on the 16.21 Speedlink service from Parkeston Quay to Doncaster. No 37.199 was photographed at Third Drove Crossing between Ely and March with ferry vans and imported cars in tow. *John C. Baker*

Right:
Section 8 grants were given to Yeomans for their busy stone terminal at Merehead. A General Motors SW1000 diesel fitted with British drawgear and retaining its American bell shunts the privately owned hoppers through a washer. In 1984 Yeomans announced the purchase of four main line diesel locomotives from the same source to operate on line-haulage work in Britain. *Chris Davis*

Right:
Since 1973, the Eastern Region had computerised its weekly train plan consisting of locomotive and crew diagrams and train workings which supplied coal to the power stations of Ferrybridge, Eggborough and Drax. From 1980, the principle was extended to other ER flows in the 'Carousel' project. No 56.008 heads east through Knottingley with a train of empty merry-go-round wagons, passing a Goole-Leeds DMU in the rudimentary passenger station. *Paul D. Shannon*

The Tyne & Wear Metro

The opening of the first stage of the Tyne & Wear Metro from Haymarket to Tynemouth on 11 August 1980 marked an important departure for urban transport in Britain. It is difficult for any visitor to the system not to be impressed by the clean, frequent and modern one-man trains which link the system's 41 stations, all unstaffed, with such an air of purpose about them.

Twenty-six miles of former British Rail tracks north and south of the Tyne were converted to Metro standards and have been linked with eight miles of new construction. Most of the latter is underground, providing much improved accessibility to central Newcastle and Gateshead; elsewhere realignments serve Byker and Chichester, whilst the Bank Foot branch was formerly open to freight traffic only.

A fleet of 90 twin-articulated 50mph Metrocars was built by Metro-Cammell for the Tyne & Wear Passenger Transport Executive. Seats for 84 passengers are provided in each unit, with space for a further 188 standing. All trains consist of two units. To demonstrate its independence from British Rail, electrification is at 1,500V dc overhead, a system which was finally eliminated from BR in 1984.

The nerve centre of the Metro is at South Gosforth where the Control Centre supervises not only the automatic signalling (trains are routed by means of coded signals set up on the cars by the drivers and transmitted by trackside transponders), but also the power supply and the station controls. A series of television monitors is used to keep an eye on the stations and their ticket machines, which are visited at irregular intervals by mobile inspectors. There is a facility for radio contact between drivers, supervisors and permanent way staff.

Below:
A pair of Tyne & Wear Metrocars led by No 4049 arrives at South Gosforth. On the right is the Metro Control Centre, while the shelter on Platform 1 shows the simplicity of the standard designs used. Through the overbridge part of another Metro train is seen arriving at the next station of Ilford Road. *John Glover*

The Metro concept requires a great deal of interchange between bus and Metro, since bus services are designed to terminate at stations with passengers continuing their journeys by train. Through ticketing on a zonal basis is the norm, whether for single journeys or period tickets. Approximately 65% of Metro users also use buses or the Shields ferry for part of their journeys.

On completion of the network in 1984 four Metrolines were in operation, each on a 10min frequency. Sone 'lines' are effectively short workings of others, and as a result the frequency in the central section is at 3/3½min intervals.

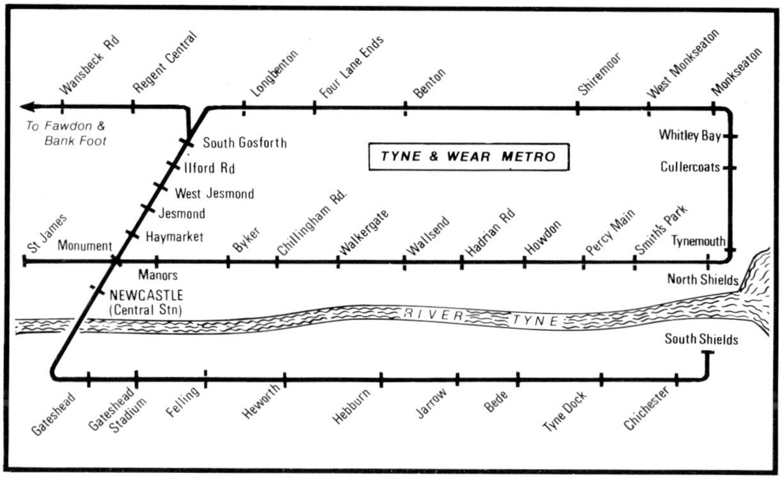

Below:
Like British Rail, Tyne & Wear PTE have some stations with rather more facilities than are required for present day purposes. Tynemouth station is totally superfluous the far side of the barriers which extend nearly to the platform edge, as is the expanse of roofing which goes with it. The use of adapted road signs such as the 'No Entry' symbol qualified by a 'Limit of Shunt' notice is typical of light rail practice. Speed restriction signs are expressed in km/h.
John Glover

1980

Left:
The 10 Class 44 diesels were all withdrawn by the end of 1980. No 44.005 is being dismantled in Derby Works, revealing the unused corridor connection fitted to the class. *Geoff Dowling*

Below:
In 1980 150 years of the Liverpool & Manchester Railway were celebrated. The London Midland's Class 86/2 locomotives which carry the names of contenders in the Rainhill trials were given a special livery containing the L&M coat of arms. No 86.235 *Novelty* leaves Rugby with the 13.00 Euston-Holyhead on 10 May.
Geoff Dowling

Left:
The Bury Interchange, providing a centrally-sited terminal for the local train service from Manchester and for PTE bus services was opened on 17 March. The 16.45 to Victoria formed of the usual Class 504 unit leaves the new station over the flat crossing which carried the Castleton-Rawtenstall freight branch. This latter was then closed on 4 December.
Kim Fullbrook

Below left:
On return from trials in the USA, the Leyland Experimental Vehicle LEV1 was sent to Ipswich and entered passenger service on 13 September on the East Suffolk line. It made excursions elsewhere, and is seen on 1 November arriving at Cambridge. Early passenger reaction was reported as favourable, with the lack of luggage space not proving a handicap.
Paul D. Shannon

Below:
The first two new stations on the 'Crosstown' Camden Road-North Woolwich service were opened on 11 June by Sir Peter Parker. A class 105 DMU arrives at Hackney Wick on an eastbound service. This was the first new inner London passenger station to be opened by British Rail on a new site for many years.
John Glover

1981

'A year of quickening productivity and of hardening priorities for change' – Sir Peter Parker

Above:
Jimmy Savile made his appearance, together with the slogan 'This is the age of the train', in 1981.

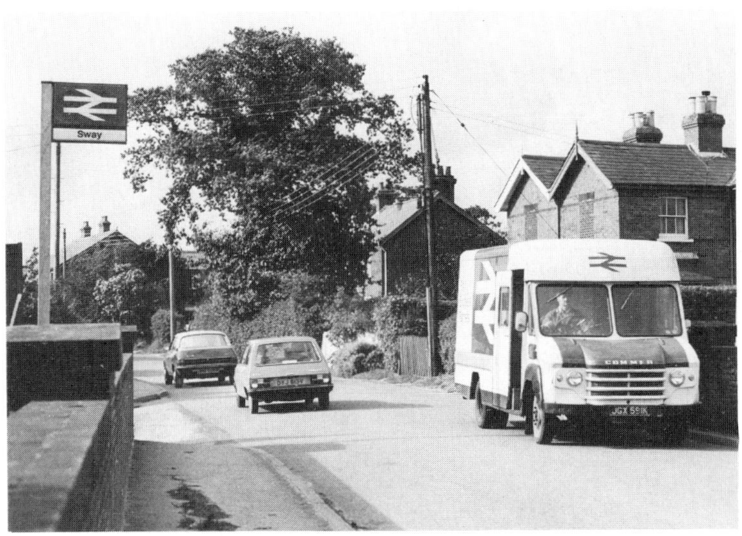

Right:
Withdrawal from the loss-making collection and delivery services for parcels took place on 1 July, and the familiar REPS (Rail Express Parcels Service) vans were seen no more. The parcels business now operated almost entirely in the quality end of the market, in sectors which were judged to have a long term profitable potential. A Commer van passes the entrance to Sway station. *John Glover*

Rail Policy

An air of desperation seemed to pervade *Rail Policy*, published in March. Bluntly, the Foreword stated that 'it highlights the critical situation which the railways now face. There must be no misunderstanding of what is at stake', and 'We ask for recognition that the issues we raise are critical for the . . . national well-being'.

The nub of the Board's case was the need for a rise in investment levels, and the document outlined a description of the feasible achievements of 1990. Following extensive electrification, Advanced Passenger Trains would be operating out of Euston, St Pancras and King's Cross, and new electric rolling stock elsewhere. New lightweight trains would be operating on rural lines, and many stations would have been rebuilt. Old marshalling yards would have been closed, and the opening of the Channel Tunnel would be imminent. The cross-London (Victoria-Euston) rail link would have been started, and staff would enjoy greatly improved working conditions. The Government would agree every investment proposal put to it, including the Stansted Airport rail link. This vision would require rail investment to rise by 85% to £567million a year on average. *The Times* described the objectives as unexceptional, and deserving of the fullest support from Government.

The renewal problems were serious enough. The age of EMUs and DMUs was one aspect of the problem, two thirds of the fleet being between 20 and 30 years old. Signalling systems, bridges, viaducts and buildings were also feeling their age. 'If', said *Rail Policy*, 'major expenditure on replacement is not started by 1983, the inevitable consequence will be a rapid rundown of the whole railway system. We could postpone until that date, continuing with some replacement and much make-do-and-mend at present investment levels, *but not beyond*'. The consequences of inaction after 10 years were said to be as follows:

Above:
Throughout the Parker years, cyclists were successively mollified and aggrieved as charges for conveyances of bicycles were removed and then selectively reimposed. Many editions of an explanatory brochure were produced, and featured Lyndhurst Road station in the New Forest on the cover.

Right:
Electrification studies all assumed a base network in which Manchester-Preston-Blackpool North was already electrified. Yet despite its apparent attractiveness as a scheme, authorisation was not forthcoming. No 47.517 approaches Kirkham and Wesham with a Blackpool North-Euston express; the diesel will be replaced with an electric locomotive at Preston. *John Glover*

Left:
Rail Policy recognised that electrification would cascade HST train sets to upgrade express services on important cross-country routes. More perhaps for political reasons, Worcester and Great Malvern subsequently received an out-and-back day service from Paddington. The 10.25 IC125 service from London makes an unlikely sight as it arrives at the staunchly GWR station of Moreton-in-Marsh. *Geoff Dowling*

- 3,000 track miles withdrawn from traffic, rising rapidly
- 800 miles carrying temporary speed restrictions (compared with 180 miles)
- Annual failure rate of mechanical signalling systems 10%, rising, (compared with 4%)
- Annual duration of train delays 8,500hr, rising (compared with 5,000hr)
- Availability of locomotives 50% (compared with 75%)
- Availability of EMUs 70% (compared with 85%)
- Availability of DMUs 60% (compared with 80%)
- Availability of loco-hauled coaches 75% (compared with 85%)

Below:
Whilst new electric rolling stock would be used on many commuter services, a discreet silence surrounded diesel operated lines with little hope of electrification. Class 207 unit No 1315, seen arriving at Eridge on the Uckfield branch, was built in 1962, while the line itself was subject to several stretches with speed restrictions due to deferred maintenance. Would the line continue to be run down? *John Glover*

Barmouth Bridge

In spring 1980, preparatory work for the replacement of seven of the piles supporting Barmouth Bridge revealed that one pile had been destroyed and another fractured by the depredations of a worm, *Teredo Norvegica*. These creatures had made a minute entry into the timber, and then bored progressively larger vertical holes within it. Closer inspection revealed that about 70 piles among the 117 spans had been attacked in this way, and a preliminary estimate put the cost of restoration work at £2½million. So serious was the threat to safety that all locomotives were barred from crossing the bridge forthwith, and diesel units were limited to 10mph.

The Cambrian Coast line is hardly a money spinner for British Rail. Annual revenue in 1981 of £304,000 was dwarfed by direct operating costs of £937,000, to which could be added signalling and civil engineering costs of £612,000 and overheads of £387,000. This was in respect of 593,000 annual journeys, of which 40% were in respect of schoolchildren travelling between Harlech and Twywn. The financial case for investing in the bridge repair, given the general lack of such funds, appeared totally unsustainable.

On 12 October the bridge was closed completely, with bus services being provided both to Machynlleth and Bangor, although the latter link (from Pwllheli) was soon discontinued. The Region authorised £300,000 to be spent on immediate repairs so that services across the bridge could be restored on 22 May 1981. 30 of the 498 piles were identified as in need of immediate replacement, and all the rest needed to be protected from attack. Total cost of restoration was put now at £1½million, made up of £800,000 to be spent on the worst affected areas in 1981, and the rest in 1982. The £200,000 cost of investigative work and the cost of immediate repairs were to be found by postponing renewals elsewhere.

So the bridge reopened amid local rejoicing, with fares and service enticements to win passengers back to rail. These were so

Right:
A Class 120 unit forms a Machynlleth-Pwllheli working having just crossed Barmouth Bridge. Initially reopened in 1981 for diesel units only, it was expected to be capable of supporting locomotive-hauled trains again by 1986. *Les Nixon*

successful that extra trains had to be brought in to cope with demand. Meanwhile, British Rail gave assurances that further repairs would be made to continue services throughout the 1981/82 winter, while the Government made it clear that the cost of repairs would have to be met from the Public Service Obligation grant.

The fracas surrounding Barmouth Bridge tended to overshadow the other problems of the Coast line. Here could also be seen the temporary speed restrictions and disintegrating signalling so graphically described in *Rail Policy*. Overall the line was becoming less serviceable and less attractive to customers, to the point at which it would one day cease to be reliable and effective transport. Nevertheless, the necessary monies were found, and locomotive-hauled trains were to be restored in 1986. 'Sprinter' units were being earmarked for local services, and a comprehensive modernisation programme involving radio signalling and automatic crossings was prepared.

Below left:
Along much of the route, the Cambrian line acts as the sea wall, keeping the coast protected at British Rail's expense. A 55mph speed restriction was in force throughout; three-quarters of the route north from Dovey Junction was laid with track 20 years old or more. The 08.15 Barmouth-Machynlleth was photographed between Penhelig and Abertafol.
David A. Flitcroft

Below:
Barmouth Harbour, with the 13.30 Barmouth-Machynlleth made up of six cars of Class 101 stock. Train lengths are determined in part by the schools traffic, for which the railway is the only practicable means of travel.
Bernard Dobbs

Review of Main Line Electrification

The final report of the British Rail/Department of Transport review was published on 11 February, and came down firmly in support of a major rolling programme of network electrification.

A base case, similar to the then current network but with the addition of the Anglia scheme, Manchester-Blackpool and Edge Hill-Earlestown, and the Ayrshire scheme was studied, together with three further options. Option 2 was a limited programme which could be completed in about 15 years and would extend the wires up the ECML to Leeds and Newcastle, down the Midland Line to Sheffield, and from York to Birmingham. In Scotland, Edinburgh-Glasgow and Glasgow-Carstairs would be electrified. When complete, Option 2 would cater for 62% of all passenger traffic and 38% of freight. The medium Option, Option 3, would add Paddington-Bristol-South Wales and Plymouth, Birmingham-Taunton, Newcastle-Edinburgh, and Liverpool-Leeds, increasing the electrically powered proportions to 75% passenger, 54% freight. Option 4 was discarded, but Option 5, the largest scheme, would add Edinburgh-Aberdeen, Doncaster/Leeds-Hull, Plymouth-Penzance and Crewe-Holyhead. 83% of passenger traffic

Right:
If a long term programme of electrification were to be embarked upon, it is a safe assumption that those line added to form Option 5 would be the last to be treated. Along the North Wales coast, a pair of BRCW Class 104 units normally employed on the Buxton line form the 11.10 Llandudno-Manchester Victoria, and were photographed leaving Abergele and Pensarn.
Larry Goddard

and 68% of freight would then be electric. For Options 3 and 5, both fast and slow rates of completion were analysed.

All evaluation was expressed in financial terms, and all Options showed improvement on the base case. In summary, the review demonstrated that a large scheme produced a better result than a small one, and that the faster the work was done, the better also the return. Sensitivity tests were employed to establish the effects of variations in maintenance and energy costs, which together made the greatest contributions to cost savings. Traffic levels, service frequency, train crew, and the cost of traction, rolling stock and fixed equipment were also examined. The conclusion was that 'it would take an unlikely combination of adverse factors to undermine entirely the prospect that a programme of main line electrification would earn a return of at least 7%'. The forecast was that the fast version of Option 5 could be completed by the year 2001.

Despite the generally accepted competence of the Review team, Government approval was not forthcoming. On 22 June, the Secretary of State for Transport 'invited BR to prepare and submit a 10-year programme of schemes only of those potentially profitable main line routes where it is clear that the benefit would justify the investment'. Approval would also be conditional on the achievement of necessary improvements to productivity'.

Sir Peter Parker put on a brave face and welcomed the response, but for many it seemed to mark a return to the piecemeal approach which took little account of network benefits.

Left:
Scottish hopes were raised by the possibility, if not the likelihood, of electrification through from Edinburgh to Aberdeen. Class 40 old-timer No 40.162 leaves Arbroath with a down parcels train. *Les Nixon*

Below left:
Penzance is served by through trains from Paddington, portion working west of Plymouth having been discontinued. Would electrification to Plymouth only under Option 3 mean the end of through services to Cornwall? No 50.021 *Rodney* arrives with a train from Bristol, whilst a London-bound HST prepares to depart. *John Glover*

DMU Replacement

Interest in the DMU replacement programme was whetted by the appearance of the Class 140 prototype, a twin-car unit with each vehicle mounted on a freight-derived four wheeled chassis. It was demonstrated on rural services around the country. In 1981 the unit underwent trial running in passenger service between Birmingham and Stratford-upon-Avon, in Strathclyde, and on the Preston-Colne and Leeds-Barnsley-Sheffield routes. Later in the year it was joined by the diesel-electric Class 210 prototype units, although the public debut of these trains was delayed until 1982.

The perceived need to provide a diesel equivalent of an EMU was the starting point for work on the replacement DMU. In 1974 BR made a decision to refurbish the existing DMUs worth saving, and use the time gained by the life extension programme to develop, test and manufacture a new diesel-electric unit to succeed them.

What became the Class 210 was aimed at the needs of commuters in the provincial conurbations. The business specification called for a high degree of passenger comfort, and performance to match EMUs, with which the new train would have to be able to run in multiple. Above the floor engine mounting was a necessity for 1,200hp, and was welcomed by the engineers. Both a three and a four-car version were produced, the price tag of £1million plus for a four-car train seemed then, as now, to debar such designs from serious consideration for widespread use.

It was always recognised that the upgrading of the DMU concept inherent in the Class 210 project would leave a gap. Whilst the Leyland Experimental Vehicle was very much a research project, the Passenger Manager's department decided to sponsor a two-car unit for service trials, as a cheaper and simpler DMU. Like the Class 210 it was to be gangwayed, but within the unit only. Despite the

Below:
The British diesel railbus story began in 1959 when 22 railbuses from no less than five manufacturers were delivered. Too small to carry an economic payload, they were withdrawn as the lines they were assigned to were closed. Some, such as this Waggon und Maschinenbau machine, survived into preservation, in this case at Sheringham on the M&GN Society line.
John Glover

Below right:
The pair of Class 210 units graduated to the Paddington suburban services, having been deemed too costly to be of interest to the PTEs. With electrification the long term aim, prospects here too seemed less than hopeful. Prototype No 210.002 passes West Ealing on the 12.30 Slough-Paddington.
Colin J. Marsden

Left:
The twin-car Class 140 unit was active in the West Midlands. On 30 July No 140.001 prepares to depart as the 10.30 Shirley to Moor Street. Considerable publicity was given to the trials, and passengers were informed on which services they could hope to find the train. *John Glover*

intention to use the Class 140 for lighter duties, it was required to meet standard structural requirements. What some claimed to be unnecessary over-engineering resulted in weight and cost penalties. The £400,000 one-off cost for two cars was said to equate to a production run cost of nearer £280,000. In 1981 it was realised that just as a version of the Class 140 could be produced for PTE use, it could just as easily be downgraded for cut price rural work. The number of DMU varieties which have followed amply bears out this expectation.

Below:
Or was it something in between which was wanted? A smartly turned out Class 101 Metro-Cammell built DMU leaves Maiden Newton with a Westbury-Weymouth service. Updates of the traditional design were later to appear as Classes 150 and 151. *John Glover*

Winter Weather and the APT Debut

In December 1981 the lowest temperatures for many years were recorded, particularly in Scotland and Northern England. It was sheer bad luck for APT, which made its inaugural run in revenue earning service between Glasgow and London on 7 December. Leaving Glasgow Central at 07.00, it arrived in Euston one minute early at 11.14 after stopping at Motherwell and Preston. Sadly, this was the only journey to be completed without incident; on the return run after unscheduled stops and a tilt failure on one coach, the train arrived back in Glasgow 30min late. On the next run on 9 December, extremely low temperatures froze moisture in the brake pipes and the train was terminated at Carstairs, whilst on the Friday, the third day of official running, lighting problems affected the train soon after leaving Glasgow. These were caused by icing on the pantograph. The train continued south, reaching Crewe 2½hr late, and was terminated there due to weather conditions. It set off back to Glasgow with a full passenger load, but failed through loss of power supply near Preston.

Heavy falls of snow were widespread throughout the country, with Wales and the West Country badly affected. Services were maintained on all principal routes, but some subsidiary lines remained closed for many days. Extreme temperatures disabled diesel locomotives, including 30% of the Scottish Region fleet. This

Below:
Two APT units stand in Shields Road depot, No 370.005 'bonnet up' and 370.002. After a disastrous debut (from the PR viewpoint at least), the trains were quickly removed from the public eye so that further modifications and trials could begin again.
Les Nixon

led to an inability to provide heating or water for toilets on steam heated Mk 1 stock, and this included sleeping car services.

Together with the snow, the low temperatures exposed the fallibility of point heaters relying on gas, which accounted for two thirds of those installed on the system. At times, Paddington, Euston and Waterloo were all closed for many hours, affecting large numbers of passengers. Communication problems were also highlighted, whether between staff or staff and passengers, and this only compounded the general chaos and dissatisfaction. Whilst rail management lambasted the thoughtlessness of passengers who descended from their trains in the Waterloo approaches to walk the remaining distance with the third rail for company, it was admitted that for a matter of hours there had been no indication of when, if ever, the trains would move again.

Above left:
Class 308 EMU No 152 disturbs the snow as it arrives at Hatfield Peverel on a Liverpool Street-Colchester service on 21 December. Services were severely disrupted by heavy snowfalls throughout the area.
Kim Fullbrook

Below:
Snow on the Pennines found 'Deltic' No 55.009 *Alycidon* between Mossley and Greenfield hauling the 13.05 Liverpool Lime Street-York on Christmas Eve 1981. All the remaining 'Deltics' were withdrawn from traffic nine days later on 2 January.
Larry Goddard

1981

Above:
The trees are covered with hoar frost as No 45.013 leaves Cambridge with a Whitemoor-Temple Mills freight on 10 December.
Kim Fullbrook

Right:
At Thurlstone on 11 February, locomotives Nos 76.035 and 76.037 were photographed hauling a westbound MGR train, the traffic most frequently associated with this route. By then, Woodhead was the only remaining BR example of the once standard 1,500v dc system of electrification. Unlike their more powerful Class 77 cousins which were sold to Netherlands Railways, the 1950-built locomotives were sent for scrap. *Les Nixon*

Above:
1981 also saw the end of the Class 306 units built for the Liverpool Street-Shenfield services, themselves built for dc traction but converted to ac in the 1960s. Unit No 089 was photographed near Romford. *Brian Morrison*

Left:
On 5 January Dronfield station reopened and within 12 months built up a regular clientele of 200 travellers. Local authority revenue guarantees were found to be unnecessary. During the winter weather the numbers were swollen to 650, and Inter-City trains were stopped specially to cope. In this picture, a six-car DMU conveying Sir Peter Parker, BR officials and local schoolchildren arrives back after a celebratory tour to commemorate the reopening. *Les Nixon*

Right:
On the opening of the Humber Bridge, rail services to New Holland Town and Pier stations were discontinued. A new service operated direct to Barton-on-Humber, connecting there with a Hull-Barton-Scunthorpe bus service. New Holland passengers were provided with a new station. A refurbished Class 108 DMU from Cleethorpes arrives at the old Pier station, which was joined by continuous platforms to Town.
Les Nixon

Below:
Vigorous opposition to the closure of the Woodhead route succeeded only in delaying its closure by six weeks until 18 July. Representing un-needed capacity, and freight only since 1970, the losses were put at £2½million a year due in part to the inefficiencies inherent in changes to and from electric traction. One of the Class 76 locomotives which was not converted to multiple operation, No 76.040, hauls eastbound hoppers on the climb to Woodhead on 3 July.
Larry Goddard

1982

'A hard year for British Rail, unnecessarily hard on our customers'. – Sir Peter Parker

Below:
The Venice-Simplon-Orient Express was inaugurated on 28 May with a train of restored Pullman cars operating from Victoria to Folkestone, connecting by ferry with a Boulogne-Venice train of CIWLT sleepers. Running only twice a week, this left plenty of opportunity for charter work for the British train. No 33.056 *The Burma Star* was photographed at Hanwood on the Cambrian line with a train to Newtown chartered by the Mid Wales Development Group.
Geoff Dowling

New Sleeping Cars

January saw the first stage in the major upgrading of the quality of overnight travel between London, Northeast England and Scotland, when the first pair of trains formed of British Rail's new Mk 3 sleeping cars entered service between King's Cross and Aberdeen. Built at Litchurch Lane Derby by BREL, the vehicles were the first of a batch of 210 which in the following two years were to supplant the whole of the existing sleeping car fleet.

The new cars offered substantial improvements in comfort, of which air-conditioning was only the most obvious example. Construction was basically similar to other Mk 3 designs, with the cars air-braked and electrically-heated. Market research had established the relative importance with which passengers rated various aspects of sleeping car travel. In descending order of importance these were: general cleanliness of the compartment, the comfort of the bed, the smoothness of ride, the noise level, washing facilities, ventilation, heating, toilet facilities, morning tea/coffee service, the convenience of the arrival, berth vacation, train departure, train boarding times, steward service, nightcap service, and reception at departure. Whilst only certain of these desiderata could be met through a new build of sleeping cars, it was clear that the then generally satisfied users would not remain so if the Mk 1 vehicles remained in service indefinitely. Also of significance was the finding that the majority were prepared to pay a higher fee for an improved sleeper facility.

Two vehicle types were built; one a 13-compartment version (SLE – Sleeper, Either Class), the other with 12 compartments and an attendant's pantry (SLEP – Sleeper, Either Class, with Pantry). One vehicle of each type works as a pair, with one attendant covering both cars. All compartments have a second upper berth which can be folded down for double occupancy, and this is the distinguishing feature between 'first' and 'second' class sleeper travel. For family use, doors between adjacent compartments can be unlocked. Vehicles are limited to 100mph; smoke detectors are fitted throughout, and retention toilets have been installed.

Below:
Durham was covered in snow as the 22.30 King's Cross-Aberdeen sleeper arrived six hours late on the morning of 14 December 1981 behind No 55.007 *Pinza*. The last six vehicles consisted of Mk 1 sleeping cars built between 1957 and 1964. *Paul D. Shannon*

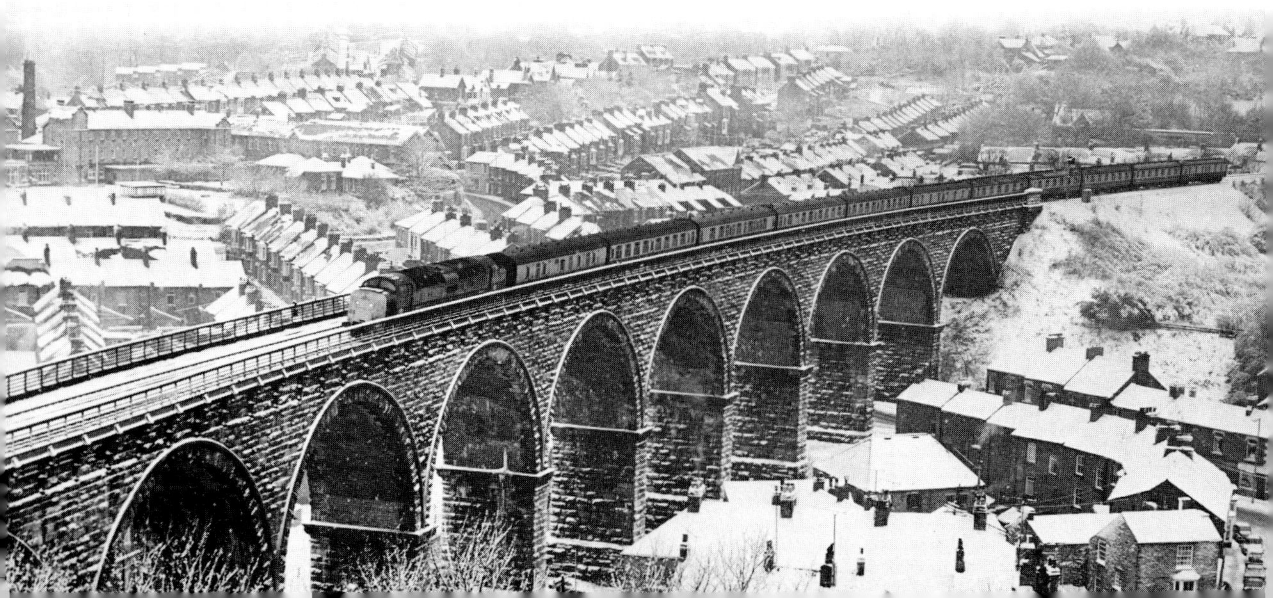

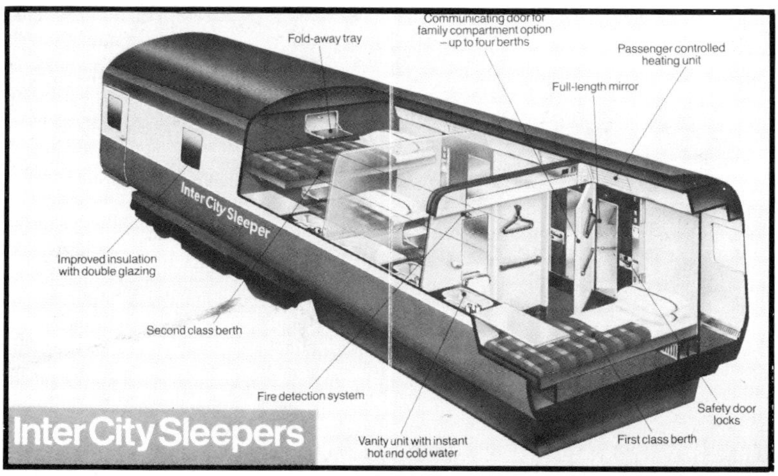

Above:
The 22.00 Aberdeen-King's Cross bowls along in the early morning July light near Arlesey behind No 47.410. This seven-car formation (excluding brake vehicles) contains 87 compartments; even if all were to be made up as second class with two berths the total train capacity is only 174 persons. The implied economics for a service competing with Shuttle aircraft and high speed daytime trains are somewhat alarming. *Michael J. Collins*

Above left:
The Mk 3 sleepers gave little clue externally to their interior appointments, and a cutaway drawing featured in promotional literature.

Left:
On the West Highland Line, No 37.039 and *ETHEL 2* leave Fort William with the 17.40 sleeper for Euston. To enable Class 37 locomotives to haul the trains with Mk 3 sleepers, a means of providing electric power to the train had to be found. Class 25 No 25.305 was one of three locomotives converted to a mobile ETH unit as No ADB 97251, and is seen here behind the '37'.
Les Nixon

Industrial Strife

Far right:
Support for the ASLEF strike was variable. The 17.30 King's Cross-Peterborough ran on many days as a DMU formation of up to 12 cars. On 16 July it was a 10-car formation and was photographed climbing past Holloway.
Martin Higginson

Below:
At Aberdeen, Clayhills sidings, there were no movements. A failed Mk 3 sleeper is stabled between a pair of HSTs. *Cyril Lofthus*

Following the loss of services for 17 days in a series of strikes in the first six weeks of 1982, caused by management's refusal to pay a backdated 3% pay increase to footplatemen on the grounds that a productivity agreement had not been honoured, a further dispute arose in June. On 29 June, in response to an announcement by British Rail that variable-day rostering for train drivers would be introduced from 4 July without trade union agreement, the Executive Committee of the Associated Society of Locomotive Engineers and Firemen called upon its members on BR to strike indefinitely from midnight on Saturday 3 July.

The strike lasted until Monday 19 July. Throughout the dispute, roundly 10% of normal services were operated, though the effect was extremely patchy. Lack of ability to predict in advance which services would operate resulted in the passenger trains that did run doing so empty, or nearly so. The dispute was ended by British Rail agreeing to withdraw its threat to sack strikers and close the

network, to treat rosters already posted at 71 depots as provisional, and not to introduce further new rosters before 2 August. In return, ASLEF terminated the strike and recalled their delegate conference, which was recommended to authorise the Executive Committee to negotiate and conclude an agreement.

British Rail estimated that industrial action in 1982 cost the industry £170million. During the strikes, many commuters in the cities took to their bicycles, motorcycles or cars, whilst others sampled commuter coach services established since the passing of the 1980 Transport Act. Employers also hired coaches; vehicles from South Wales and Cornwall were observed on such work in London, and Sealink UK Ltd hired coaches to convey 'Boat Train' passengers. Other scheduled services operated by National Bus Company subsidiaries were augmented, as were British Airways' shuttle services. Golden Rail holidaymakers were particularly hard hit, as were hotel proprietors participating in the Golden Rail scheme.

Industrial users of rail still managed to move their goods; in the oil industry some precautionary building up of stocks had been undertaken in anticipation. Neither the Post Office nor the Newspaper Publishers Association had any reservations about the use of rail again after the dispute, as both relied on the sophisticated and integrated distribution which rail can supply for large and regular amounts of traffic. Other industries were more cautious both from their own point of view and that of their customers. Whilst investment in privately owned wagons and private siding facilities may have tied industries to rail for the time being, different attitudes might prevail when contracts came up for renewal.

For British Rail, the priority was to rebuild confidence in all market sectors. By the year end, passenger volume had recovered to within 10% of 1981, while both freight and parcels achieved an operating surplus before interest despite the drop in revenues.

Below left:
'Autumn Leaves' was the title of an apologetic leaflet issued by the Southern in 1982, explaining with the aid of these drawings why the problem was still unsolved in the 1980s. A subsequent production was entitled 'Snow'.

Below right:
The London Connection was an early example of joint marketing by British Rail and London Transport of their services in the London area, following the determination of their respective chairmen to improve matters.

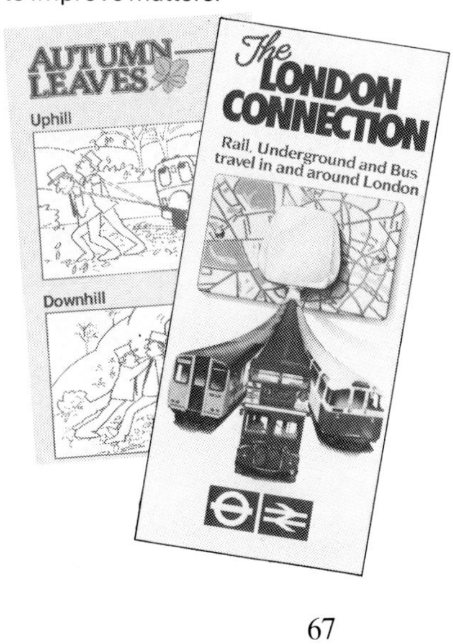

The Parcels Business

The parcels business contributed about 7% of the railway's commercial revenue in 1982. It was heavily dependent upon three traffics:

- the Post Office letter mail and parcels contracts, which together produced about 40% of revenue;
- premium parcels traffic (mainly Red Star), producing about 25% of revenue; and
- carriage of newspapers and periodicals, contributing a further 25% of revenue.

General parcels traffic, including livestock, perishables and Continental traffic was therefore limited, following in part from the withdrawal of loss-making collection and delivery services the previous summer. The parcels business now operated almost exclusively in the quality end of the market; here customers required frequent, fast and reliable transits, and rail is in a strong competitive position to provide these.

In 1982 there were two contracts with the Post Office. The letter mail contract had run since 1930, and was for a fixed price (updated for inflation) for an unlimited volume of mail. The parcels contract was based on a price per bag for individual flows. Both traffics, but particularly parcels, had declined significantly in recent years due to Post Office mechanisation reducing the number of sorting offices (which made road movement more economic) competition from air services, and a shortage of space in some trains (HSTs for example). Nevertheless, with 4,000 trains carrying mail daily, including 43

Below:
Class 86/2 No 86.242 *James Kennedy GC* heads south at Grayrigg with a long train of parcels vans. Behind is the M6 motorway, a continuing threat to all rail business on the northern end of the West Coast line. *Brian Morrison*

Travelling Post Office services every night, parcels remained big business for British Rail.

Red Star provides a station to station service on scheduled passenger trains which may be nominated by the customer. In November 1982, Red Star was supplemented by Night Star, an overnight service which included delivery by private carrier. It offered late acceptance times and delivery by noon the following day to nearly 700 towns, and a money back guarantee in the event of late delivery. The market was highly competitive, and Red Star had been losing ground heavily to both motorway-using road hauliers and the Post Office.

Newspapers are a perishable commodity, and British Rail carried about 12 million copies every night. Distribution by rail accounts for 70% of the market, and as with the TPOs, the train journey includes sorting en route so that parcels can be made up for individual retail outlets. Some periodicals are less time sensitive and this traffic was largely road based, but 'Magstar' was being developed to provide a disciplined low cost service using surplus rail capacity.

Above left:
Exhibition trains are part of the parcels sector; most are constructed around superannuated Mk 1 coaching stock. This creation was no exception, and was built for the benefit of KP Nuts. Photographed at Waterloo, it would have made an even more remarkable picture if it had been caught by the photographer as it was propelled up the main line. *Colin J. Marsden*

Below:
After waiting patiently for an hour or so for a path, No 25:191 leaves Birmingham International with a single parcels van. Payloads have to be extremely profitable if they can support the cost of running a train by the contents of just one van! *John Glover*

Heavy Freight Locomotives

The first Class 58 Co-Co diesel-electric locomotive, No 58.001, was handed over to Railfreight at a ceremony at Doncaster Works on 9 December. First of a batch of three similar locomotives, orders for 95 were anticipated, but these were later cut back to 50 as a result of the NUM strike. Its appearance broke completely with British tradition. The class was also the first to be turned out in the new Railfreight livery of grey superstructure, yellow and black cabs, red painted underframe and buffer beams, black bogies and full height BR logo.

Class 58 evolved from what in 1973 was perceived as an urgent need for a purpose built freight locomotive to cope with an expected upsurge in coal and other block load freight traffic in the wake of the oil price crisis. The immediate response was to design and build a locomotive drawing heavily from a proven design; this strategy resulted in the Class 56. That locomotive followed the Class 47, but with a new power unit, a Ruston Paxman 16RK3CT rated at 3,250hp. Built solely for freight haulage, with slow speed control for merry-go-round coal duties and no train heating facility, the Class 56 has enjoyed considerable operational success. However,

Below:
No 47.406 became test-bed 47.601 when it was fitted with a 16-cylinder Ruston RK engine prior to its use in Class 56. In 1980 the locomotive was re-engined for a second time with a prototype of the 12-cylinder engine to be installed in the Class 58. Renumbered No 47.901, it is seen in this latter guise at Westbury depot.
Brian Morrison

construction costs were relatively high, added to which maintenance problems were encountered due to restricted access space within the body shell. The Class 56 construction programme extended to 135 units, which were delivered between 1976 and 1984.

The main objectives of the Class 58 design were as follows:

- Economy in construction.
- A minimum overall maintenance requirement, with easy accomplishment of whatever maintenance might be necessary.
- A facility to adapt to export markets with a minimum of modification.

Design was based on a simple underframe formed of rolled steel joists with a non-load bearing superstructure, compared with the monocoque design of the Class 56. The new locomotive was essentially a cost cutting version but retaining the well proven power specification and power equipment. The result was a capital cost saving of around 14%, and whilst construction cost of the first pair of locomotives was said to have exceeded £3million, series production reduced the cost per locomotive to £800,000. A Ruston 12-cylinder RK3ACT engine, itself directly descended from the engines fitted to the LMS diesel locomotives Nos 10000 and 10001 but now rated at 3,300hp was fitted, with Brush electrical equipment. The weight in working order was 130 tonnes and the maximum speed 80mph.

Below:
Class 56 locomotives see regular use on stone trains. No 56.045 carefully brakes its train of 1,500 tons of roadstone as it slows for the junction with the West of England main line at Witham. The train is on the branch from Merehead quarry, and its destination is Westbury sorting sidings.
Geoff Gillham

Bottom:
Class 58 No 58.014 eases out of Birmingham Lawley Street Freightliner terminal with the 20.15 to Felixstowe. These locomotives are built solely for freight haulage, with slow speed control for merry-go-round coal duties and without train heating facilities. Up to three locomotives may be operated in multiple.
Geoff Dowling

West Coast Infrastructure Review

If a high operating performance is expected, the infrastructure must be capable of allowing it. The purpose of the infrastructure review was to establish what needed to be done in engineering terms to allow for present and future traffic flows and 125mph train speeds, and how work could be coordinated. The result was not an investment plan as such, but rather an indication of how several proposals could be implemented for little cost as part of the programme of routine renewals. Clearly, this was an engineering-led exercise, seemingly with little business justification. Initial work concentrated on the West Coast line from Euston to Carlisle, and amongst others it covered proposals relating to:

Fast lines: permanent speed restrictions
The basic line speed was 100mph throughout, but there were no less than 68 permanent locations where speed had to be reduced. Where an improvement was considered feasible, a recommendation was made. The most severe check was to 20mph through the Crewe station area.

Slow lines: permanent speed restrictions
Because daytime 'weaves' between Euston and Rugby were a standard operating feature, and to cope with a future three-speed-band railway (125, 100 and 75mph) necessitating the transfer of some 100mph trains to the slow line on a planned basis, the maximum slow line speed was recommended to be raised to 100mph.

Secondary/diversionary lines: permanent speed restrictions
While the scope for upgrading line speeds between Rugby and Stafford via Birmingham was limited, the section between

Below:
In the Bletchley area it was proposed that when the crossovers between fast and slow lines became due for renewal they would be replaced by new 70mile/h parallel two-way junctions at Bletchley South. Modifications to the track layout would affect proposals for resignalling; in the long term the LMR saw 10 power signalboxes only controlling the WCML, with none between Willesden and Coventry/Nuneaton. The 07.40 Euston-Birmingham New Street hauled by a Class 86/2 locomotive passes under the flyover at a steady 100mph. *John Glover*

Bushbury and Birmingham could be raised to 100mph without capital expenditure, but only if adequate weekday maintenance possessions could be provided. The speed between Walsall and Rugeley should revert to 60mph so that excessive delay could be reduced when trains were diverted over this line.

Simplification/relocation of junctions

In the electrified area there were still a large number of junctions which incorporated switch diamonds or which needed to be relocated to improve the reliability of train working and simplified to minimise maintenance costs. Wherever possible these should be replaced by a series of single leads.

Signalling policy

Modifications to the track layouts would obviously affect proposals for resignalling. In the long term, the London Midland Region foresaw the West Coast network being controlled from 10 power signalboxes only.

Reversible working

To facilitate track maintenance on two tracked sections by regular mid-week maintenance possessions where there were no additional tracks available for trains to 'weave', facilities for reversible working were recommended. However, it was neither possible or financially justifiable to superimpose reversible working on existing signalling, and such facilities could only form part of long term signalling strategy. Reversible working requires like for like signals on both lines so that trains can be flighted on the 'wrong' line at full speed.

Electrification of diversionary routes

There were a number of non-electrified secondary lines within the West Coast electrified area which were used as diversionary routes. Because of low line speeds and the need to stop to attach/detach diesel locomotives, there were unnecessary additions to journey times. The spread of network electrification would reduce the number of diesels available for such work. Infill electrification was seen as a means of overcoming these problems.

Below:
For many years BR and indeed its LMS predecessors had considered a major remodelling of the track layout in the Crewe area, which had remained unchanged since steam days. The extent of conflicting movements is demonstrated by No 47.447 arriving with the 13.09 Holyhead-Euston and effectively blocking other movements at the north end of the station. At the same time, trains on the through lines were restricted to 20mph.
A. Wyn Hobson

Right:
The view south from Crewe shows the equally complex layout. Class 86 locomotives heading the departing 09.20 Blackpool North-Euston and the 09.00 Euston-Carlisle cross each other. Track remodelling, which involved a virtual shut-down of the station area for seven weeks took place in summer 1985. A new signalbox was built, fast line speeds were increased to 80mph and points and crossings reduced from 229 to 106, diamonds from 56 to four. *A. Wyn Hobson*

1982

Right:
Milton Keynes Central, three miles north of Bletchley, was opened by HRH Prince Charles on 14 May with public services commencing three days later. The station was built at the behest of the City's Development Corporation, which provided more than two thirds of the finance. Local services previously terminating at Bletchley were extended, whilst a selection of InterCity trains call. Traffic growth has exceeded all expectations. A Class 86/2 accelerates away towards Euston
John Glover

Left:
A partial service of High Speed Trains was introduced to St Pancras on 4 October. Five trains covered 13 journeys each weekday, following a reassessment of earnings potential for the 95-train fleet. HSTs were expected to increase Midland revenue by £5million a year, equal to a 15-20% increase in passenger carryings. This was offset by £1million loss of revenue on the routes from which the HSTs were drafted away. A crew-training run emerges from Belsize tunnel consisting of three redundant TRUK catering cars and a Guard's Trailer Second.
John Glover

Below:
The Basic Interval Timetable came to Scotland on 17 May. Starting at Edinburgh as the major interface with Anglo-Scottish traffic, standardised timings at fixed minutes past the hour giving a repetitive pattern of working were applied progressively throughout Scotland. Even the Highland line was brought in, with northbound departures from Perth at 00.50. The 09.15 from Inverness to London King's Cross was photographed at Dalwhinnie. *Les Nixon*

Right:
The Papal visit to Britain commenced on 28 May. No 73.142 *Broadlands* was turned out to haul the four coach special from Gatwick Airport to Victoria. Pope John Paul II travelled in the Southern Region General Manager's saloon next to the locomotive, and the headcode 'HF' was displayed for Holy Father. The number of special trains laid on to take crowds to the various public appearances was unprecedented in postwar history. *John Glover*

Centre right:
The Ayrshire electrification at last got the go-ahead from Strathclyde Regional Council following a grant from the European Railway Development Fund. Other funds came from the Scottish Office and BR. The scheme involved electrifying and resignalling the lines to Ayr and Ardrossan at a cost of £68million. A Class 116 DMU provides a connection with the boat for Brodick at Ardrossan Harbour, just beyond the reach of electrification.
John Glover

Bottom right:
The Southern received the first of a series of Class 455 units in November, initially for use on the South Western services. Subsequent batches were for use elsewhere on SR inner suburban routes. The new trains marked a return to all-steel construction rather than the aluminium bodywork of the PEP-derived stock, and with all the motors concentrated in one vehicle. This scene was photographed at Epsom.
John Glover

1983

'The overall result was the best for six years' – Bob Reid

Above:
The use of rail for business *and* pleasure was the theme of a general leaflet extolling the benefits of travel by the InterCity 125.

Right:
Freight closures included the former Burry Port and Gwendreath Valley to Kidwelly Junction. On 15 September, the last day of operation, Class 03 locomotives Nos 03.144/151/120 return to Coed Bach washery. These were the only locomotives allowed to work the line, and even they had to have their cab roofs lowered. Coal is now transported from the washery via Kidwelly and a new link line.
Michael Rhodes

The Serpell Report

The Serpell Committee was set up in mid-1982 'to examine the future of the railway and associated operations, in the light of all relevant considerations, and to report on options for alternative policies, and their related objectives, designed to secure improved financial results in an efficiently run railway in Great Britain over the next 20 years'. The findings were published after extensive leaks on 20 January 1983; the report was instantly derided, with most invective directed to its lukewarm approach to investment, and the future network options. The publication of network maps has long been fraught with problems. According to G. F. Fiennes in his autobiography: 'The great and good Doctor (Beeching) threw a spanner into the works causing a shower of sparks and ugly grinding noises. He had not many outward and visible signs of human frailty, but one sign was his love of maps, and another his love of publishing them'. The Commons Transport Committee was also unenthusiastic: 'Not only were the (network) options irrelevant to any sensible discussion about the future of the railways, but they were also extremely damaging to the general reception given to the Serpell Report and, indeed, did much to undermine its credibility'. The Railways Board itself called the report disappointing: 'There was very little advice on the big question of the nature and extent of the long term strategic objectives which BR and the Government should be pursuing'.

What therefore did Serpell say?

Below:
The Leamington Spa-Hatton-Stratford upon Avon service received special mention in the Serpell Committee Report. The line was identified as having revenue of £76,000 and direct costs (only) of £425,000 (1981 prices). Curiously, it survived the C1 Network Option, which was supposed 'to achieve savings by deleting the worst performing services'. A Hatton bound train approaches the deserted Claverdon station. *John Glover*

- There is scope for major cost savings in engineering: in civil engineering, signalling and mechanical engineering.
- The relationship between the BRB and BREL should change.
- There are serious deficiencies in the BRB's planning procedures.
- Most – if not all – rail investment will continue to be financed by public sector funds.
- When dealing with BR, the Department of Transport should shift away from matters of detail to matters of long term policy.
- If efficiency is vigorously pursued, a railway of roughly the present size could be operating in 1986 on a smaller PSO grant (in real terms) than that received in 1975.

Presenting a series of options on the possible shape of the rail network in the long term, the Report said:

- A railway of 1,630 route miles would be commercially viable.
- Cutting 80 route miles from the present network might save £180 million a year.
- A High Investment Option would not show a satisfactory financial return.

Alfred Goldstein's dissenting Minority Report said:

- The emphasis in the main Report should have been more on the long term.
- It is unlikely that the 1986 PSO requirement will be contained to within the 1975 level.
- The only way to make a major impact on the level of public financial support needed for the railway is to alter the size of the network.
- While agreeing with much of his colleagues' criticism of BR management, Goldstein considered that the railway could be a vital organisation serving a useful role.

In the wake of the political storm, the report was quietly forgotten. By the time that the Board's 1983 Annual Report came to be written, Serpell did not even rate a mention.

Above left:
Network Option A, the commercial railway, received the greatest public attention. A passenger deficit of £32million would be offset by freight profits and result in an overall profit of £34million. Option A contained only 1,630 route miles, or 16% of the present network. Class 421/1 4-CIG No 7334 seen in Clapham Cutting and bound for Littlehampton would have to be diverted to Brighton, although the Eastbourne line was shown as surviving.
John Glover

Above:
Engineering expenditure was criticised. For civil engineering it was said that keener prices could be obtained for new rail and sleepers, the renewals themselves could be carried out more efficiently, and that a review of maintenance levels and their manning implications was overdue. The Class 08 shunter was photographed at Oxford.
John Glover

Midland Suburban Electrification

The industrial relations problems concerning driver-only operation (DOO) of the Moorgate/St Pancras-Bedford electric services were finally resolved in March, after the trains had laid idle for over a year, and creating much public hostility in the process. Full electric services commenced in July, although on a reduced timetable compared with that originally intended, and first class accommodation was not included in the units.

The Midland Suburban Electrification scheme covered 52 route miles and 230 single track miles. The usual preliminaries were undertaken, and these included track rationalisation, the installation of power signalling controlled from a single box at West Hampstead, and the modernisation and adaptation to electric traction of Cricklewood depot. Major civil engineering work concerned the rebuilding of the branch from Dock Junction to Moorgate, with the construction of a new interchange at King's Cross (Midland) providing direct subway connections to the Victoria, Piccadilly and Northern Underground lines. In the tunnel sections to Farringdon, headroom was insufficient for 25kV traction, and the tracks had to be lowered. Ballasted track was replaced by concrete slabs for over a mile, as this minimised the construction depth required. Due to the tight clearances and sharp curvature in the tunnels, maximum speeds are restricted to 30mph. Here, as elsewhere, stations were generally refurbished or rebuilt.

The 90mph Class 317 trains were the first of a new generation of electric units. Based on the Mk 3 coach, they are however about 13% shorter due to clearance restrictions. Forty eight gangwayed four-car trains were built by BREL at Derby and York, each consisting of two driving trailers, a power car with pantograph, and a non-driving trailer. Two sets of double air operated sliding doors were provided on each side of each car, which are released and then closed by the driver. The opening of doors is dependent on passenger operated push buttons. Two controlled-emission toilets are incorporated in the non-driving trailer.

Closed circuit television is installed, with monitors at the platform ends viewable from the driver's cab. A cab to signalbox radio link is also maintained. The Inspecting Officer of Railways laid down six main requirements for DOO:

- Secure radio communications between the driver and the signalling control centre.
- Driver controlled public address.
- Power operated passenger doors with over-riding control by the driver.
- All passenger doors proved closed before traction power can be applied.
- Closed circuit television along platform for drivers.
- Means for passenger exit without assistance from railway staff.

Below:
A pictorial representation of the Midland Suburban Electrification in a brochure issued by Westinghouse Signals.

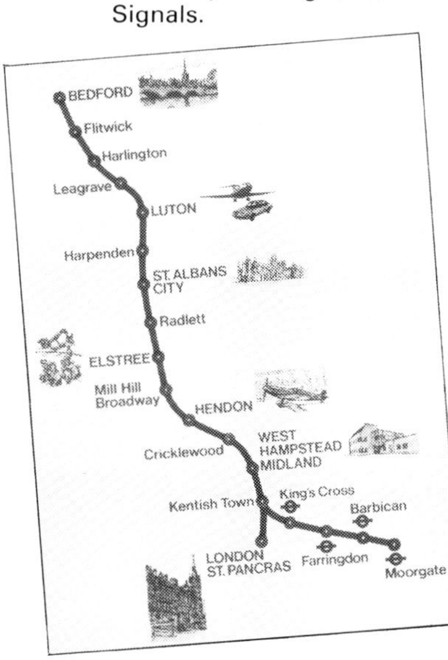

Above:
The Midland line DMUs had their lives extended whilst the dispute over Driver Only Operation of the electrics continued. With station rebuilding complete and all overhead equipment in position, a Class 127 unit arrives at Leagrave with an up local service on 21 April 1982. *John Glover*

Above left:
Leaving the rebuilt Bedford Midland station for Moorgate is No 317.311. In the foreground are the fast lines which avoid the station and which remain non-electrified. West Hampstead power signalbox controls the whole of the Midland line services as far as Irchester, 13 miles north of Bedford. *Kevin Lane*

Left:
Standing unwanted in sidings at Bedford on 21 April 1982 were Class 317 units Nos 317.314/25/26. It was not until 28 March 1983 that the first electric train to carry fare-paying passengers ran, crew training having started in mid March.
John Glover

The Selby Diversion

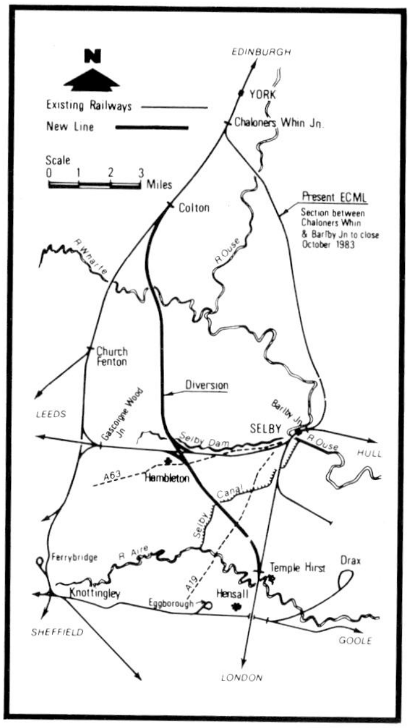

High Speed Trains between King's Cross and the north-east were routed over the new Selby diversion from 3 October. This marked the completion of the project, the planning of which started in 1976, to allow the Selby coalfield to be fully exploited without adversely affecting the East Coast main line through subsidence. The 14½-mile line, financed by the National Coal Board, provided for 125mph running throughout, and avoided the speed limited Selby swing bridge and the reverse curves north of the station.

The diversion leaves the former ECML at Templehirst Junction where a 70mph single track connection to the Selby line is retained, and the River Aire is crossed by a new steel bridge. Other water crossings are over the Selby Canal, the eight span Selby Dam viaduct, and the 525yd long Ryther Viaduct. This latter with its 26 spans carries the new line over the River Wharfe and its flood plain. There are also 13 bridges with roads under, and one over the railway, as well as other minor structures. The alignment throughout is gently curved and easily graded, and at its northern end connects at Colton Junction with the Normanton line for York via a specially designed switch diamond and turnouts allowing 125mph on both routes.

At Hambleton, the new route passes underneath the Leeds-Selby-Hull line, and two new spurs have been built. A double track link from south to west allows direct running between Templehirst Junction and Gascoigne Wood (towards Leeds). A single track spur from east to north maintains a direct Selby-York link without the necessity of routeing via Church Fenton, the former ECML route north of Selby being subsequently closed. Signalling is controlled from a new panel in the existing York box, which is one of the oldest

Below:
The flatness of the terrain is evident in this view of Class 31 No 31.143 as it heads the Bounds Green-York stock train over the Selby diversion on 12 December. *Les Nixon*

of its type and dates from 1951. The York control area is therefore extended to fringe with Church Fenton, Gascoigne Wood, Selby and Doncaster signalboxes.

At Gascoigne Wood, coal will come to the surface from five shafts. Most of the output will be burnt at Drax, Eggborough or Ferrybridge power stations. The loading terminal is built on the site of the former yard. It has two large loading bunkers for coal, and a third for stone spoil. A steady flow of trains is planned; when full production is reached in 1988, two 1,000 tonne trains should be leaving Gascoigne Wood every hour, each having taken only 15min to be loaded.

Above:
Selby swing bridge and the associated curves imposed an increasingly severe speed restriction as line speeds generally were raised towards 125mph. The proposal to divert the main line away from Selby thus enabled the Eastern Region to avoid costly upgrading work. On 17 September in the last week of the 'old' main line, an up HST for King's Cross negotiates the swing bridge.
Les Nixon

Left:
At Chaloner's Whin south of York, an up IC125 takes the Selby line as a Class 47 approaches with a King's Cross-York semi-fast. The four tracks lead to Sheffield and Leeds, but also nowadays to Colton Junction which is the northern end of the Selby diversion.
Les Nixon

Government Objectives for British Rail

On 24 October 1983, British Rail received the clearest set of objectives it had had for many a year. Main feature was the achievement of a reduction in the dependence on the Public Service Obligation grant to £635million a year (1983 prices) by 1986 rather than 1988 as suggested in BR's own corporate plan. Adjustments were made to the 1983 PSO at the same time; of the total of £819million, £147million was in respect of the InterCity sector, £266million for London and South East Services, and £406million for Provincial Services.

The Secretary of State told British Rail that 'the guiding objective should be to run an efficient railway, providing good value for money. Services to your customers should be reliable, attractive and punctual, at acceptable fares and charges; and the cost to the taxpayer should be reduced. That is the way to achieve a secure future for the railway, enable worthwhile investment to go ahead and give your employees satisfaction and pride in their work.'

The letter went on to state that it was not the Government's intention that there should be a programme of major route closures, but that views on bus replacement schemes would be welcomed.

Below:
The Board's views were sought on the practicability of introducing some guaranteed and subsidised substitute bus services, where they would be appropriate on local transport and value for money grounds. Two Midland Red West vehicles under contract to British Rail are seen at Kidderminster awaiting the arrival of a Class 116 DMU from Worcester, ready to take passengers to Blakedown by road during planned engineering work on Blakedown viaduct. Rail-bus connections are usually much less convenient.
John Glover

Commercial remits for InterCity, Freight and Parcels were redefined and emphasised. A review of BREL was to be undertaken, and privatisation options pursued there, as well as in supply and support services, including rail and station catering.

These were the messages for British Rail's new Chairman, Bob Reid, who took over in September. Reid had already pointed to the creation of Sector Management, introduced in 1982, as a prerequisite to forming a business led organisation. He too had stressed the need for investment, but his central theme was self-sufficiency. 'Years of practical experience as a railway manager . . . have convinced me that the less dependent an industry is on any source other than the paying customer, the more efficiently it will run. The way to prosper in any business is to satisfy the customer by giving value for money.'

Left:
Excess capacity in BREL was to be rationalised as soon as possible, with future options to include privatisation. Railway rolling stock was to be provided by competitive tender whenever possible. No 58.025 was photographed under construction at Doncaster Works. *Colin J. Marsden*

Below left:
Punctual this train was not, but the service was attractive. Due to train staff shortages, travellers from Euston had had no refreshments all night, so the West Highland section decided to prolong the morning stop at Crianlarich so that passengers could get out, stretch their legs, and have a cup of tea. As No 37.111 waited at the head of the 21.50 Euston-Fort William, the passengers, probably unused to this sort of treatment, relaxed in the soft Highland air. The tearoom has since closed. *Cyril Lofthus*

The Docklands Light Railway

Plans for the redevelopment and regeneration of London's Docklands received a substantial fillip following Government approval for a light rail system to serve the area costing £77million. Utilising sections of the former London and Blackwall Railway and the North Greenwich branch, together with the North London Railway route to Poplar, the majority of the system was to be on existing railway rights of way and carried on brick arches above ground level. Notable new construction will be the bridges across the dock areas themselves, with stations on the intervening wharves.

The City terminus is to be at Minories, beside the Fenchurch Street station throat. Passenger access is less than ideal, with 2½min estimated as the walking time to Tower Hill Underground station, but the project budget is insufficient to allow better arrangements. Running at first parallel to the British Rail line, the route diverges

Below:
The Docklands Light Railway's City terminus at Minories will be at viaduct level between the railway and the multi-storey car park from which the picture was taken. Class 302 unit No 303 leaves Fenchurch Street with a mid-morning train to Shoeburyness. Docklands trains will run side by side with Eastern Region services as far as Stepney East before branching off towards the Isle of Dogs. *John Glover*

past the Regent's Canal Dock and to the quay area, site of the operations and maintenance centre. Routeing thence is either north to Stratford BR/LRT station, or south to the Island Gardens terminus. Trains will run on segregated tracks throughout.

The initial system will have 16 stations, all unstaffed but with television monitoring. Up escalators are to be provided for stations at viaduct level, together with lifts for the disabled. The contract to build and equip the railway was won by a consortium of GEC and John Mowlem. It covers design, construction, associated signalling and control equipments, the stations, depot and 11 articulated and automatically controlled electric light rail vehicles. Control of the trains will be centralised with data processors linked to the trainborne and trackside control and safety equipment. Controllers will oversee the operation and be able to speak to attendants travelling on the vehicles, and to passengers at stations. Services are to run every 7½min from both Tower Hill and Stratford to Island Gardens.

Completion of the scheme, which is being overseen by London Regional Transport, is guaranteed for July 1987. Meanwhile, planning work was progressing on a Stage II scheme to extend the line east to Beckton.

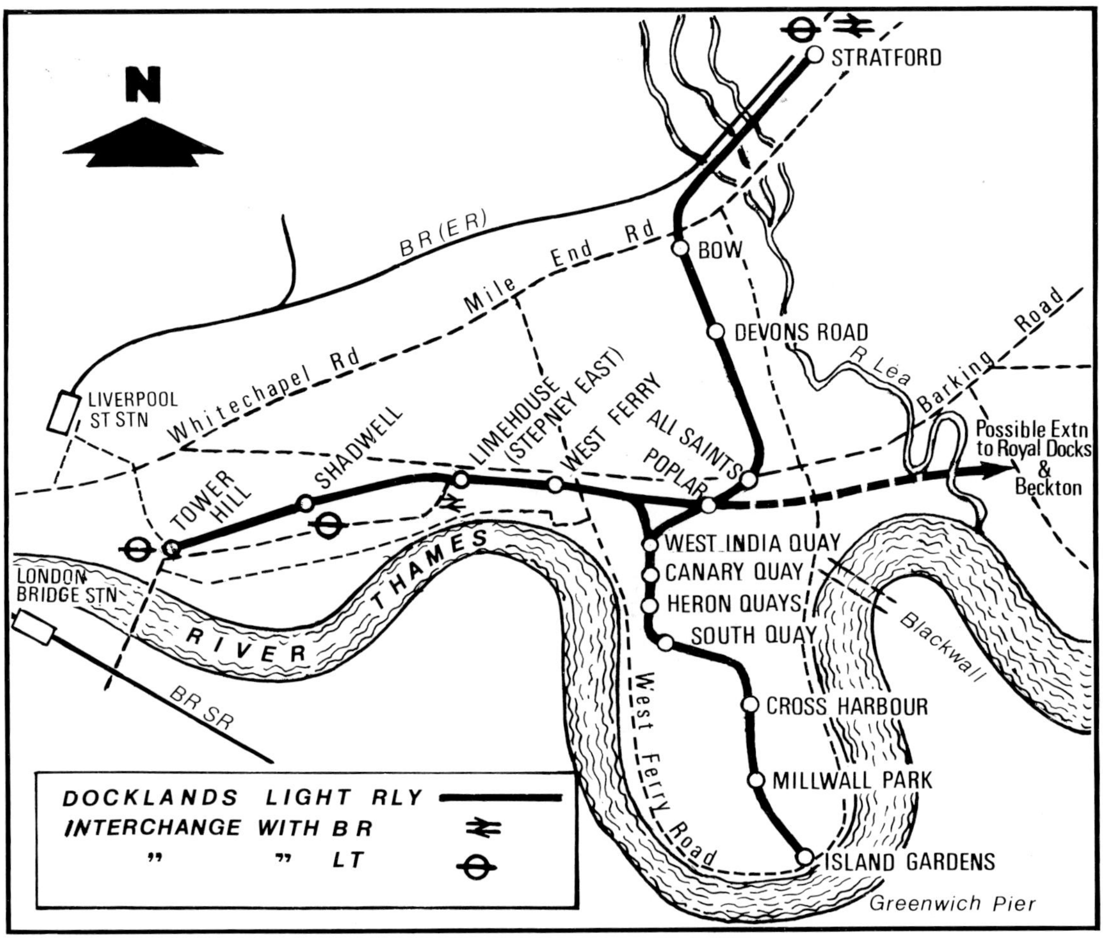

1983

Above:
A new look for Inter-City was launched on 28 September as part of an 'Executive' package; two Western Region HST sets and the Manchester Pullman were reliveried in two tone grey with red and white lining for the occasion. There were also new internal decorative schemes. Set No 253.030 leaves Bath Spa with a Paddington-Bristol working. *Les Nixon*

Above right:
The long hot summer of 1983 brought many examples of overheating power cars on HST sets caused by excess coolant consumption. With the leading power car shut down, the 11.45 Paddington-Penzance is assisted through Newton Abbot by No 31.288 on 30 August.
Geoff Gillham

Right:
Passenger closures included the little lamented Elmers End-Sanderstead service in South London. On 13 May the last train of six cars with Class 415/1 No 5209 at its head explodes a succession of detonators as it leaves Selsdon on the final return journey. *John Glover*

Top left:
Consent for the closure of the Dalston-Broad Street line was also given, but subject to new facilities being provided into the rebuilt Liverpool Street via a new curve at Hackney. Meanwhile, the bulk of the service was to be diverted to Stratford and North Woolwich using lines newly equipped with the third-rail, and operated with Southern Region Class 416 units. A Class 501 has just left Dalston Junction for Richmond, while a DMU waiting in Dalston Kingsland Road station will shortly depart for Camden Road. *Colin J. Marsden*

Above left:
New liveries began to appear on PTE sponsored services, with the Strathclyde black and orange appearing first on the Class 314 units bought for the Argyle line. Units Nos 314.209 and 303.042 were pictured at Helensburgh Central in the new colours, while No 303.071 retained blue and grey. *Chris Davis*

Left:
The Mk 1 coaches used on the Glasgow Central-Stranraer Harbour boat trains began to sport a new livery of signal red upper half with light, medium and Trafalgar blue lower panels in 1983. A corresponding livery was applied to the DEMUs of Northern Ireland Railways, used on the Larne-Belfast Boat Trains. No 47.098 leaves Ayr with the 07.45 from Stranraer Harbour, which connected with the 03.30 boat from Larne. *Paul D. Shannon*

Right:
The condition of Goole swing bridge over the River Ouse prompted a closure proposal from BR for the six miles of line between Goole and Gilberdyke. Doncaster-Hull trains would have been diverted via Selby. The estimated cost of repairs was put at £2million, and eventually these were largely funded by Humberside County Council. Class 105 and 108 DMUs cross the bridge on a local service.
Les Nixon

Below right:
The reconstruction of Southampton Tunnel commenced on 12 March, in an operation which was expected to take up to five years but which was completed in half that time. Commercial requirements dictated its continued use by trains, although only a single track would be made available; freight trains were mostly diverted via Salisbury. At the western end of the tunnel, with the contractor's narrow gauge track in the foreground, No 33.048 emerges wrong line with the 13.10 Portsmouth Harbour-Bristol Temple Meads on 11 August.
Geoff Gillham

Right:
The extension of third-rail electrification from Tonbridge to St Leonards was authorised in October at a cost of £24million, and this will bring about the withdrawal of the narrow 'Hastings' DEMUs. Class 201 No 1005, one of the original batch on short underframes, hurries through Elmstead Woods with the 15.45 from Charing Cross. Diesel traction will then be eliminated from a route, half of which had been electrified for 20 years or more. The singling of the lines through the three tunnels with restricted clearances will enable standard electric stock to be used.
John Glover

Above:
'Cornish Railways' was created with its own management team based at Truro, as part of the planned reorganisation which saw the end of the Western Region Divisions the following year. As part of the new image, St Blazey depot adorned No 37.207 *William Cookworthy* with a lizard logo on the side and a coat of arms on the nose. It is seen passing Lostwithiel with a down engineers' train.
Brian Morrison

Right:
A resignalling scheme to eliminate one of the larger remaining semaphore signal strongholds was authorised for Leicester. No 45.106 passes Leicester North box with a St Pancras bound train. *John Glover*

Right:
Plans were announced for lowering the annual payment Strathclyde makes to BR for operating rail services. 24 miles of new electrification, new signalling centres to be built at Yoker and Paisley, Driver Only Operation of trains, open stations and automatic ticketing, rationalisation of depots, minor closures and track singling made up the package. The Class 107 DMU heads a six-car formation into Fairlie with a Largs-Glasgow Central service. This line would be singled and electrified.
John Glover

Below:
Electrification to Hunt's Cross enabled the stopping service from Manchester to Liverpool via the former Cheshire Lines Committee route to be terminated at Hunt's Cross for much of the day, with passengers continuing their journeys by electric trains. A Class 507 unit calling all stations to Kirkby leaves, while the Class 108 DMU in Platform 2 prepares to depart for Manchester Oxford Road. *John Glover*

1984

'We need to redouble our efforts to keep our customers and find new ones' – Bob Reid

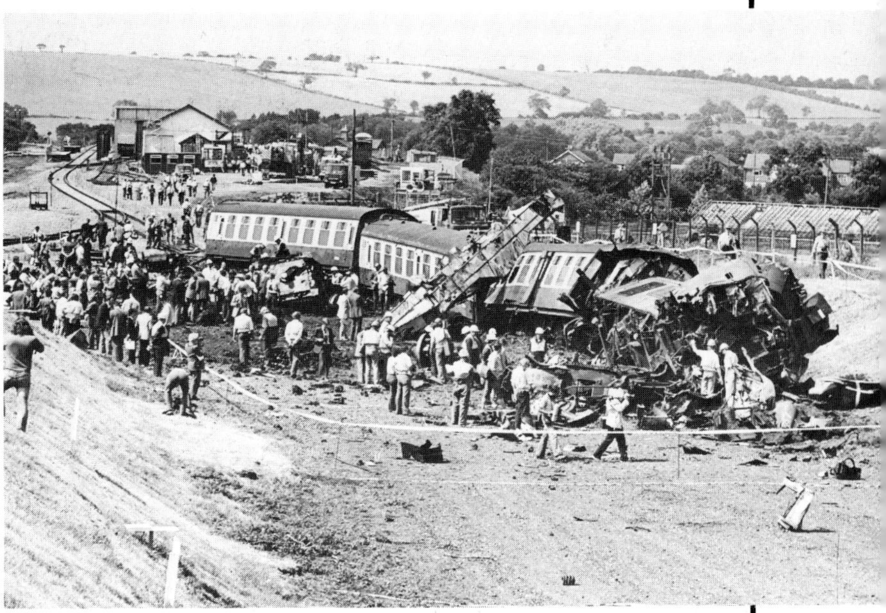

Right:
In an orgy of destruction, the Central Electricity Generating Board purchased Class 46 No 46.009 from British Rail and three Mk 1 coaches, and ran them full tilt into a nuclear flask and Flatrol wagon in an attempt to demonstrate the indestructibility of the flasks. The exercise was carried out on the Old Dalby test track on 17 July before an invited audience at a reported cost of £1.6million. The remains of the wagon and its load (which survived as forecast) were subsequently put on show at the NRM. This view shows the aftermath with the wagon lying on the first coach. The relative lack of damage to the rolling stock was notable.
Colin J. Marsden

Rails into Roads

British Rail commissioned consultants Coopers and Lybrand to undertake a study into the merits of converting closed or underused railways into roads, to see if there was indeed evidence that this might be in the public interest. Ten route sections in the London area, both radial and orbital, were studied.

The emphasis of the study was on the profitability to the Railways Board, assuming (a) the Board would gain the financial benefit of conversion, (b) that closure consent would be forthcoming for the lines concerned, (c) that adequate investment funds would be available for conversion and the diversion of rail traffics to other routes, and (d) that the PSO grant would not be affected. The Steering Committee considered the costs of conversion and the diversion of rail services, providing alternatives, and the revenue loss as a consequence of service withdrawal. These costs were set against the railway operational and infrastructure savings, plus a projected revenue (by tolls or payment by Government in lieu of tolls), and the value of time savings for traffic using the roads.

The Steering Committee's report concluded that 'conversion would produce roads which are not only below the standard laid down for primary urban distributor highways, but have widths and

Below:
The approaches to Marylebone station with the fuelling depot beyond the Class 115 DMU suggest that plenty of land would be available in the station vicinity for a road, but that Lord's tunnel in the background and other tunnels beyond would impose severe restrictions upon the road's capacity. If Marylebone were to close, the Underground would provide all services to Amersham; an A60 stock train from Baker Street can be seen disappearing into the Metropolitan Line tunnel. *John Glover*

characteristics which are outside the parameters recommended by the Department of Transport for any all-purpose limited access two way through roads'. Even with a lower design standard, three routes were still ruled out, and the parts of the Great Central line beyond Northolt were considered to have too little road traffic potential. This left Cricklewood-Kew-Barnes and the West London line where the benefits were at best only marginal, and Marylebone-Northolt as the only prima facie case worth study. Two options presented themselves: either a route for cars only, or as a dedicated busway but restricted to single deck vehicles due to tunnel clearances.

On the same day in March, British Rail announced that they intended to close Marylebone station and withdraw all services. High Wycombe/Aylesbury trains would operate from Paddington, and a shuttle service would operate between Aylesbury and Amersham only. This service would connect with Underground trains to Baker Street. The decision to seek closure was said to be unrelated to the 'Rails into Roads' study, and also to the National Bus Company's plans to turn Marylebone station into a coach station. The purpose of that scheme was to relieve pressure on Victoria coach station, and also to provide an unimpeded exit from central London via a busway link for coaches only. From the railway point of view, the NBC would be just another potential purchaser for surplus assets.

Above:
Road-rail cooperation is not limited to urban areas, as the promotion in 1984 of the Derbyshire Day Discoverer ticket shows. This inexpensive ticket at £2.50 for an adult and £5.00 for a family also gave discount admission to many attractions.

Left:
Wembley Complex has enjoyed modest success as the station for the Wembley Exhibition Centre, with trains making a non-stop run to Marylebone in 10 minutes. Wembley Complex, Sudbury & Harrow Road, and Sudbury Hill Harrow will close if the High Wycombe service is diverted to Paddington. Long after the centre tracks were removed as surplus to requirements, a Class 115 arrives with an up afternoon train.
John Glover

Manchester Plans for the Future

The Manchester rail system is characterised by its complete lack of any link between services north and south of the city. Competition between the railway companies which built the system resulted in a number of terminal stations; those that remain are Piccadilly and Oxford Road to the south, and Victoria to the north. All three are situated on the edge of the central business district rather than in the heart of the city.

Past rail improvement schemes have ranged from the effective but costly Picc-Vic tunnel to the cheap and nasty Castlefield Curve, but no work was done on either. In 1984 more radical ideas were afoot, although whether all will survive the upheaval of local government reorganisation and the restructuring of the bus industry remains to be seen.

There are three schemes. The first is to construct a new chord line between the Piccadilly-Buxton line and the former Central-St Pancras line, allowing the operation of through Sheffield-Liverpool services via Stockport and Manchester Piccadilly. Faster journey times will be offered and Stockport, a major traffic source, will be served. The cost of the Hazel Grove Chord scheme is being met from internal funding by BR.

British Rail also proposed a scheme linking Piccadilly through platforms Nos 13 and 14 with Preston via a southeast-northwest curve from the Earlestown line to the Bolton line at Windsor Bridge to the west of Salford station. This scheme allows the operation of through services from the north of the conurbation to the south and the closure of large parts of Victoria. It is associated with 25kV

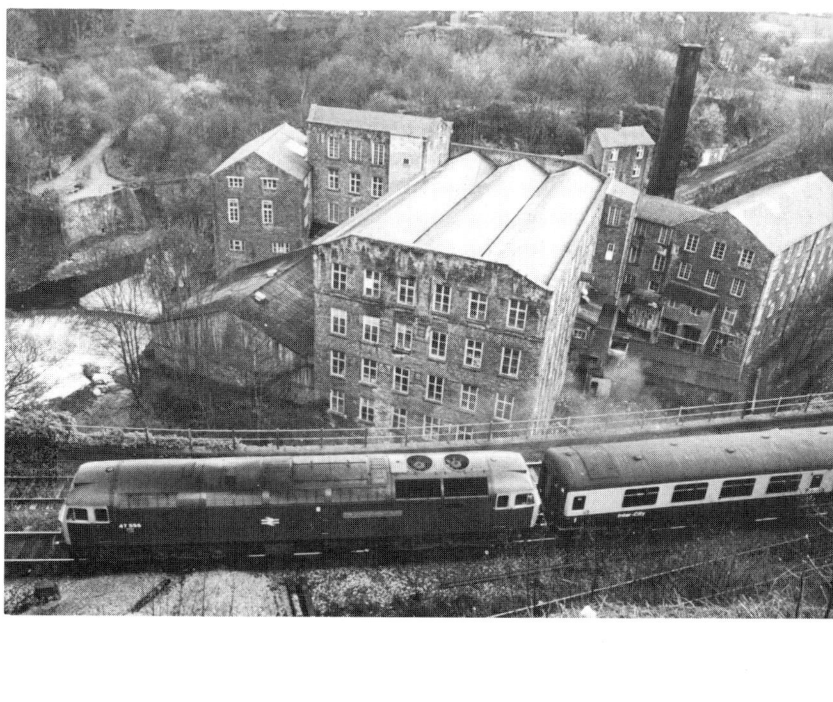

Right:
'The European' was introduced in 1983 as a through service between Harwich Parkeston Quay and Edinburgh/Glasgow Central. In the Manchester area the train approaches via the Hope Valley route from Sheffield and thence via New Mills Central to gain acess to Victoria and then continue to Bolton. With the Hazel Grove chord and the Windsor Link in place this train would then be rerouted via Stockport and Piccadilly. On 16 April the southbound train headed by No 47.555 *The Commonwealth Spirit* is about to enter New Mills tunnel. *John Glover*

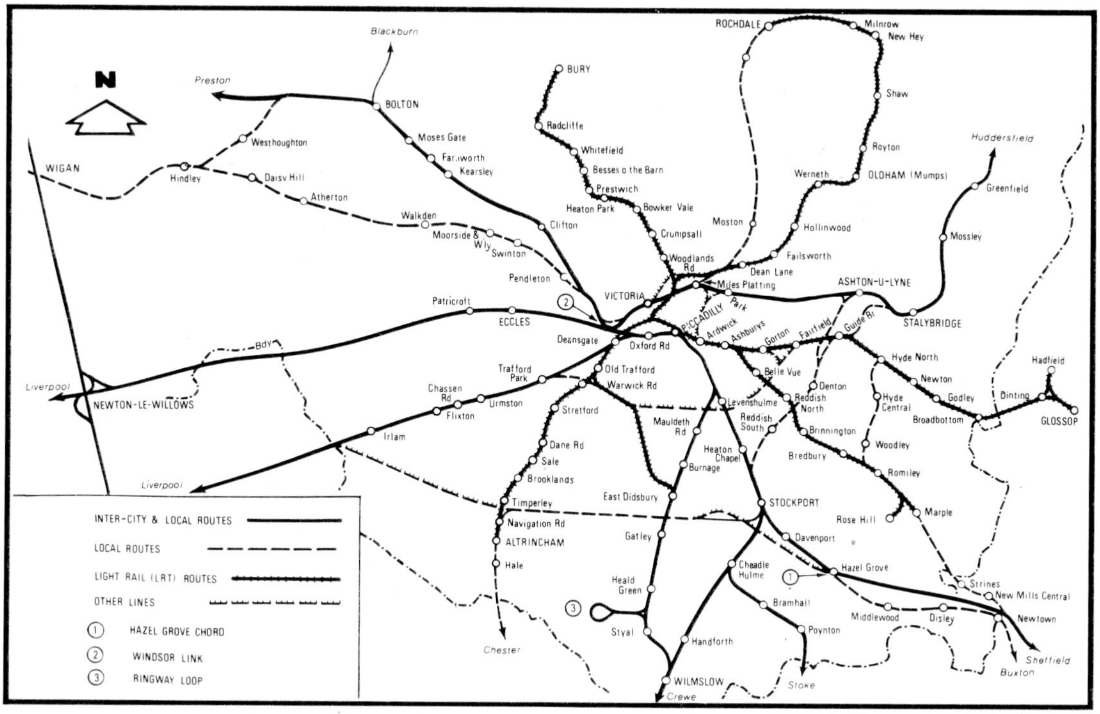

electrification between Manchester and Blackpool North, allowing not only through Manchester-Glasgow electric haulage, but also eliminating traction changes on Blackpool-Euston services. The total scheme costs of £32million include property purchase and demolition, building the link, and electrification throughout. Funding would come in part from Greater Manchester Council (£7½million), Lancashire County Council (£2½million), and British Rail (£22million). Provision of the Windsor Link, so far without electrification, was authorised in 1985.

Notwithstanding these links, Manchester's local rail system is now in need of a large dose of investment funding if a network of the present extent is to be kept running into the next century. Rolling stock, signalling and infrastructure are all in need of renewal. The favoured solution is a Light Rail Transit scheme, converting services to Bury, Oldham/Rochdale, Marple, Hadfield, Altrincham and the presently closed line to East Didsbury into an LRT system. Most of the network would be reserved for LRT, but with some limited freight movement. In central Manchester there would be street running, with LRT tracks set in the highway surface but separated from road traffic as far as possible. DC overhead current collection would be used. Maximum speeds of 60mph would be reduced to 30mph in the city. Two-car articulated units able to use both pavement level and conventional platforms are envisaged, operating from Bury and the (now disused) Reddish depots. The result would be an impressive upgrading of the quality of local rail services, and much improved journey times through better access to the city centre.

Finally, Ringway Airport might be linked into the rail system by a loop off the Styal line.

Right:
Marple is one of the proposed terminals of the light rail system which would provide an ideal means of development and renewal of the life expired assets of the local railway. Rolling stock would be two-car articulated units of generally continental design and appearance. From Marple the journey time to Piccadilly would be reduced from 25 to 17 minutes, with the added attraction of through journeys to the City Centre. A Class 108 arrives on the 13.20 from Manchester.
John Glover

Below:
The Class 506 units on the Glossop/Hadfield services were finally phased out on 7 December, after which the system was converted to 25kV ac traction; they were replaced by Class 303 units transferred from Glasgow. Hybrid unit No '06' takes the Hadfield line at Dinting South Junction. If the LRT plans come to fruition, it will be necessary to convert back to 1,500V dc, the chosen traction system.
John Glover

Gatwick Express

The expansion of Gatwick Airport and the rise in associated rail use has been encouraging for the Southern Region. The resignalling of the Brighton line together with major civil engineering work at locations such as Gloucester Road Junction, Croydon, have made a number of desirable improvements to the way and works. The ageing 4VEG units used on the Rapid City Link services were not a strong selling point, and crowded trains catering for a mixture of commuters, day visitors to the South Coast, and airline passengers often with much luggage and little English made uneasy bedfellows. Such were the prospects for further traffic growth and the financial benefits that this was expected to bring, that plans were made for a major revamp of Central Division services from May 1984. For the London-Gatwick traffic there were four planning criteria: segregation of airport traffic, a major uplift in the quality of the rail product, improved passenger handling, and a margin to meet further traffic growth.

The key was new equipment. The spread of High Speed Train operation elsewhere had made redundant good quality air-conditioned Mk 2 stock. Haulage could be effected by taking up spare time in the Southern's fleet of Class 73/1 Bo-Bo electro-diesels, provided push-pull working with the rolling stock could be arranged. This was essential, because of the service frequency and the short duration of the journey. The solution was found in the adaptation of 10 driving motor brake seconds from former 2HAP units. Seats were removed to create ample van space, but other facilities have been retained. Seventy-seven locomotive-hauled coaches have been modified and formed into permanently coupled two and three-car units. Tables have been removed from the open

Below:
14 May saw the introduction of the 'Gatwick Express' service operating non-stop from Victoria. No 37.123 was repainted in matching InterCity livery to the rolling stock and given the name *Gatwick Express* for the occasion. It is seen leaving Victoria on 24 May with the 11.00 departure. In the first year of operation, passenger journeys increased by 33% to 4 million.
John Glover

seconds as have eight seats, to create easier access and to provide luggage space. The vestibule doors have been converted to automatic operation. Leaving Victoria, trains are normally formed of locomotive, eight trailers including one first class vehicle, and the van. All vehicles have been repainted in the new InterCity livery.

Trains operate every 15min on the 30min journey from 05.30 until 23.00 from Victoria, and from 06.20 until 00.05 from Gatwick. Allowing for terminal layover time, seven sets are in constant use. Trains are serviced at Stewarts Lane; the night service is provided using ordinary EMU stock.

Below right:
The Rapid City Link was a short term expedient to try and make high-density stock more appropriate for use on an airport service. In each unit 30 second class seats were removed and replaced with luggage racks, and the adjacent windows painted over. The conversions were carried out in 1978 on standard 4-VEP stock which became Class 427 (4-VEG). They have since reverted to standard. A Driving Trailer Composite was photographed at Haywards Heath. *John Glover*

Below:
At the London end of the train will be found a thinly disguised 2HAP vehicle, now classified as a Class 489 Driving Motor Luggage Van. No 9109 is at the head of train No 5 in the circuit as it approaches Clapham Junction. *John Glover*

Rural Railways Review

In spring 1983, the Association of (shire) County Councils and British Rail joined forces to examine the future of the rural railway system, the most marginal part of rail operations. It was agreed to conduct a joint submission to the Secretary of State on these major points:

- a fresh look at engineering, operating and safety standards, signalling and maintenance on rural lines to allow the retention of a low cost railway;
- the establishment of clear rules for bus substitution with effective financial guarantees and appropriate transfer of resources from BR to counties; and
- further discussion of the financial ground rules, especially on the costing of passenger services on lines which would otherwise only carry freight.

Many facets of operation of the rural railway were examined. The resources required to run a rail service, such as the infrastructure, rolling stock and staff, are all determined by the service pattern. Hence BR must seek to meet market requirements as closely as possible at the lowest operational cost. Results can be optimised by having good management information, which includes the assessment of market needs.

Above:
Scarborough Borough Council were responsible for producing a local timetable describing the Esk Valley line to Whitby in 1984.

Left:
Traditional token exchange is taking place at Wroxham as the 09.21 Sheringham-Norwich arrives formed of a Class 105 DMU. The Working Party looked forward to radio signalling which, it was expected, would match present safety levels but at far less cost. One control centre only on each line would maintain radio contact with each train driver and use an electronic 'token'. Projects were under way on the Kyle line and the East Suffolk. *John Glover*

Right:
A smartly turned out Class 104 DMU arrives at the semi-derelict Blackpool South station. The Working Party considered that much more could be done to help BR maintain the public parts of their property, even down to such mundane levels as lighting and sweeping stations as part of normal street services.
John Glover

Typically local rail services only require simple forms of stations and ticketing. Items such as provision of car parking or ticket machines which record journey details were additional facilities which could be the subject of joint County Council/BR ventures. Similarly there may be opportunities for special arrangements with local authorities over the lighting and maintenance of some stations.

BR has a legacy of historic structures, often unsuitable for current requirements, which it is required to maintain. This duty was seen as deserving special financial recognition. The statutory procedures applied to minor resiting of stations are excessively cumbersome, and some rationalisation of the closure arrangements for these cases was considered necessary.

The infrastructure determines the costs involved in its renewal and maintenance. Consequently, rationalisation to match the resources more closely to current traffic requirements was seen as a worthwhile means of keeping the costs of rural railways down. Other obligations, such as the requirement to maintain sea defences, go beyond the needs of BR for running trains and were seen as an area deserving of special financial arrangements. Fencing of railways alongside arable land or in remote areas was seen as not always necessary.

Above:
The value of a railway is related to the traffic it generates from its catchment area. In 1984, a single Class 121 unit operating only every two hours was judged sufficient to cater for the traffic from Rhymney to Bargoed, where connections were provided for Cardiff. The branch train, which made only one return journey of 5½ miles each way in the two hour period, was pictured during one of its periodic slumbers at the Rhymney terminus.
John Glover

Many lines still had traditional mechanical signalling systems which are expensive to staff and maintain. At the same time, there has been insufficient financial return to justify replacement with remotely controlled modern power signalling schemes. Development of computerised radio signalling now enables substantial savings to be realised. Even simpler systems warranted further appraisal.

Overall, BR had an excellent safety record. However, safety is only achieved at a cost which, if pursued too far, may lead to line closures. Road users accept much higher levels of risk. Refinements in safety procedures, for example at level crossings, may marginally improve on an already very safe system, but at disproportionate cost. Automatic level crossings were not only more cost effective than manually controlled barriers, but also had a better safety record.

The methodology of bus substitution, should attempts to revive individual railways fail, was examined, with recommendations that bus links should be designed to fulfil specific purposes rather than being general in character. Discussion of the 'Speller' Act whereby experimental services can be introduced, and subsequently withdrawn without resource to statutory procedures, led to hopes of greater flexibility in financing requirements.

APTIS and Friends

Towards the close of 1982, it was announced that approval had been obtained for British Rail to invest in a three-year programme to replace all the existing manual and mechanised systems of ticket issue.

There are three main items of hardware. First, there is the All-Purpose Ticket Issuing System (APTIS) which is to be installed in all 1,600 BR staffed ticket offices, and for which 2,971 machines were required. For conductor guards and others issuing tickets away from offices, 1,750 Portable Ticket Issuing System (PORTIS) machines were to be acquired. Finally, Passenger Operated Machines (POTIS) were to be introduced, starting with an experimental Agiticket System machine at London's Charing Cross and a Pinpoint credit card machine at Euston.

The key feature of the new system is the APTIS machine. Developed by BR engineers in conjunction with Thorn-EMI, the machine is more a computer with ticket issuing ability than a straightforward ticket machine. In its memory are stored fares for all BR ticket types for 2,500 destinations, plus 250 London Underground stations. This includes fares for alternative routes.

Right:
Some of the tickets issued from various machines and in use in 1984; 1 Edmonson card (preprinted); 2 Flexiprinter (with rubber overstamp); 3 Rapidprinter; 4 Ultimatic; 5 Setright; 6 NCR 21; 7 Almex; 8 Handiprinter; 9 Omniprinter; 10 NCR 51; 11 Westinghouse-INTIS; 12 Thorn-EMI APTIS.
John Glover

The 24 most popular destinations are available by pressing a single key; otherwise the clerk needs to input the first four letters of the name, eg *Earl* will produce *Earlestown*, but this can be advanced by a single key to *Earley, Earlsfield, Earlswood (Surrey)* and *Earlswood (West Midlands)*. Keying in of ticket type then produces the fare. Tickets are normally printed on blank stocks held within the machine, but the clerk may insert other blanks for use for Season Tickets for instance. Data is also encoded on the ticket by magnetic stripe, checkable by the use of verifiers issued to ticket inspectors, but used also for operating barriers on the London Underground.

Using a telephone and a modem link, each APTIS machine is interrogated daily by the central computer at Nottingham to extract the results recorded for the day on magnetic tape. Current analysis of ticket sales will be available for management purposes. The same link is used in reverse, when the central computer updates the APTIS machine memories for fares changes.

The PORTIS machines are simpler, with a limited fares memory but performing similar functions. They are accessed by a Data Retrieval Unit at the end of each day and the information transmitted to Nottingham.

1984

Left:
The end of the Trans-Pennine Class 123/4 DMUs in May was hastened by the presence of asbestos, which has to be eliminated either by withdrawing or stripping out the vehicles concerned. A Class 123 Driving Motor Second leads a Doncaster-Sheffield local service out of Mexborough. *John Glover*

Below left:
In a blaze of publicity connected with the TV programme, power car No 43002 in HST set No 253.001 was christened *Top of the Pops* by Jimmy Savile OBE at Bristol on 30 August after a record breaking run from Paddington in 62min 33sec. Five trailers only were used in the formation, and the driver was given dispensation to run at 130mph. No 253.001 was photographed at Bishton near Severn Tunnel Junction on 26 October with the 10.01 Swansea-Paddington. *Geoff Dowling*

Right:
Authorisation was received in January to electrify from Bishops Stortford to Cambridge. No 37.050 rounds the curve at Bethnal Green with the 14.06 Kings Lynn-Liverpool Street. Realignment work was to be undertaken on the newly electrified lines to raise the ruling line speed from 75 to 90mph. It was hoped to provide an hourly electric locomotive hauled service to Cambridge in 1987.
John Glover

Below right:
Silkstone Common station opened on 26 November. Funded by South Yorkshire County Council, the station is situated on the single track Barnsley-Penistone line. The line itself was reopened to passenger services in 1983, when Sheffield-Huddersfield services were diverted via Barnsley on closure of the direct route. Passenger traffic increased by 40% as a result. The line beyond Penistone remains threatened with closure. A Class 110 DMU finds some traffic with the 11.08 Huddersfield-Sheffield on 28 December. *Les Nixon*

Below right:
Despite a generally improving safety record, 1984 was marred by a series of spectacular and highly destructive accidents in which a number of people lost their lives. On 4 December, the 10.05 Liverpool Lime Street-Scarborough collided violently with the rear of the slow moving 09.00 Stanlow-Leeds oil tanks at Weaste, Salford. The driver of the Class 45 locomotive No 45.147 and two passengers were killed. That the death toll was not higher was perhaps a reflection on the general paucity of passenger traffic, as the front two coaches were gutted by fire. In this view, photographed the same evening, the debris is being cleared. *Kim Fullbrook*

Left:
The first Class 150 made its press debut on 19 November and was well received. All the Class 150/151 prototypes were to be based at Derby Etches Park, together with the first 50 production versions ordered from BREL. Officially marketed as the 'Sprinter', No 150.001 found immediate employment on the Matlock branch, and is seen here at the terminus.
Les Nixon

Below left:
The sad remains of Bedford St Johns, at one time an important intermediate station on the Oxford-Cambridge line, were finally closed in 1984. The remaining service, from Bletchley, was diverted to Bedford Midland and a new station provided on the connecting link. A Class 104 unit awaits departure from the former premises.
John Glover

Bottom right:
The MAGLEV scheme commenced operation between Birmingham International station and Birmingham Airport. The 680yd long double track line runs about 30ft above ground level and there are terminal platforms at first floor height inside each of the termini. Passengers are conveyed in linear-induction powered cars each with a capacity of 40 passengers with luggage. The £3million project is a joint development between West Midlands County Council, British Rail and private industry. In this picture, a vehicle approaches the airport. *John Glover*

Right:
New liveries continued to appear, ranging from the highly successful to the bizarre. This (depot level) treatment of No 25.322 which also resulted in its being named unofficially *Tamworth Castle* was described disparagingly as 'ice cream van livery'. It is seen at Bletchley TMD in October. *John Glover*

Below right:
Other Eastern Region electrification schemes were authorised which together with the closure of Stratford-Tottenham Hale would have the effect of eliminating DMU operation at Stratford. Both the Romford-Upminster and Wickford-Southminster branches were approved for low cost schemes. A Southminster branch train leaves the intermediate station of Althorne on its return to Wickford.
John Glover

Bottom right:
The Greater London Council funded an extensive programme of station improvements. An Underground station to benefit was Baker Street where the original 1863 built platforms were restored to their former Victorian style. Sodium lighting deputised for daylight which formerly entered by the shafts in the tunnel ceiling. A 'C' stock Metropolitan Line train for Hammersmith is arriving.
John Glover

Left:
The restoration of a regular passenger service to the Leeds-Preston Trans-Pennine route via Copy Pit summit was marked on 1 October by a civic launch at Hebden Bridge. The service of six trains each way (five on Saturdays, no Sunday service) followed a single return journey which had been operating since May provided on the initiative of the National and Provincial Building Society. It is marketed by the London Midland Region as 'Roses Rail Link'. A Class 101 DMU was working the 10.40 from Leeds when it was photographed on 31 December at Portsmouth, south of Copy Pit summit. *Les Nixon*

Below left:
The first of the 15 trains of '1983' Underground stock entered service on the Jubilee line; a six-car train awaits departure from the Charing Cross terminus. Construction follows established practice of steel underframe, conventional traction control and all-rubber suspension. All these features will be radically different in the new generation of stock for the Central Line replacement programme and for which prototypes have been ordered. *John Glover*

Left:
Transport within the site of the Liverpool International Garden Festival was provided by a 15in gauge railway. The service between Herculaneum gate and Play Centre station was sponsored by British Rail and provided by the Ravenglass & Eskdale Railway's *Silver Jubilee* diesel unit. Decked out in the latest BR InterCity colour scheme, it is seen passing the public house – one of the few permanent buildings on the site. *John Glover*

Below:
The 1983 plans for Strathclyde included the immediate introduction of improved services between Kilmarnock and Ayr, half-hourly Glasgow-Barrhill and hourly Glasgow-Kilmarnock from May 1984. Kilmaurs and Auchinleck stations were also to be reopened. It was hoped to introduce Class 150 diesel units to these routes in 1987, but in the meantime Class 27 No 27.030 and three Mk 1 coaches formed the 12.40 Carlisle-Glasgow Central on 28 August, and was photographed at Auchinleck. *Les Nixon*

1985

'The railway can be in a much better shape at the end of the decade' – Bob Reid

Above:
Saver tickets were introduced selectively to combat coach competition, but were amalgamated into the basic fares system in May 1985. The slogan is now 'We're getting there'.

Right:
Various overtures were made regarding privatisation of train services. Sea Containers, owners of Sealink UK, planned to conduct a feasibility study into running the Isle of Wight railway as a private concern. Class 485 4-VEC unit No 485.041 leads the 12.30 Ryde Pier Head-Shanklin south from Brading. The oldest Underground cars on the system were built in 1924, and the newest in 1935.
Brian Morrison

InterCity – Into Profit

Financial targets set for the InterCity business required profitability by 1989. With revenue worth over £500million in 1984, InterCity was set for a tough £103million turnround; plans to meet the remaining £29million shortfall were to be decided later. A strategy document was published, showing a 16% income growth, with expenditure trimmed by 4%.

Market research had confirmed that InterCity speed, safety and comfort were generally acknowledged. But people thought also that railway staff were unhelpful, that trains were dirty and overcrowded, and that the railway was difficult to use by the uninitiated. Analysis showed that leisure travel at £200million was worth a little more in revenue than business travel, with obligatory journeys such as commuting of less importance.

Five business groups have been identified: West Coast, East Coast, Western, Cross-Country and Midland. The latter three were the weakest, with relatively higher costs per train mile and lower earnings; together they accounted for 78% of the losses and only 36% of revenue. Indeed, to meet the financial target, the Cross-Country group (Northeast/Northwest to South/Southwest/South Wales) needed to improve earnings of around £8 per mile by 85%. Conversely, the East Coast had the smallest gap between costs and revenues, and was expected to improve further with electrification. Neither the market or the competitive situation was constant by route, but a profile of an average train mile showed earnings at £9.57 and costs at £12.44:

Below:
The InterCity strategy laid stress on the need to provide direct services from the south and west of London to the West and East Coast main lines, and options included the restoration of the existing Snow Hill tunnel between Farringdon and Blackfriars and upgrading the West London Line. No 47.486 was heading for the latter as it approached Sevenoaks with a return charter train to the London Midland Region.
John Glover

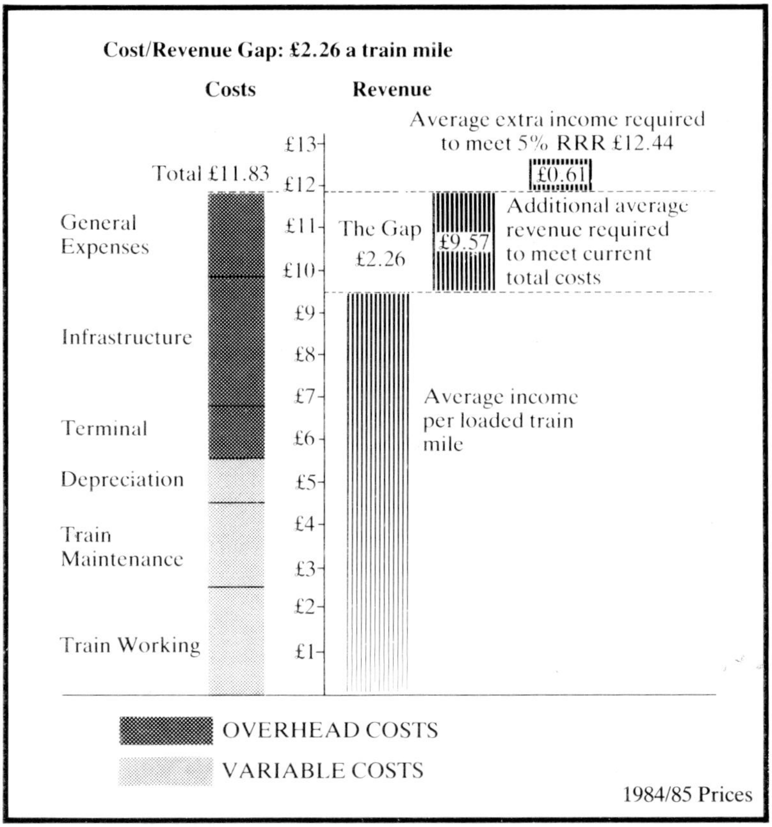

Below:
The summer peak is still evident in the West Country, and InterCity was intent on improving the utilisation of its resources. At Bristol on a June Saturday, 47.613 *North Star* is about to depart at 10.05 with the 07.50 Swansea-Penzance, only to be followed four minutes later by No 45.179 with the 07.17 Derby-Penzance at 10.09. If such services are to be maintained economically this can only be done by withdrawing stock from use elsewhere. In 1985 London-Birmingham services were reduced on Saturdays for this purpose. *John Glover*

A four point strategy was devised to close the gap:
Redefinition of the network meant that some local services were to be transferred to the Provincial Sector, while London-Ipswich/Harwich/Norwich were gained from London and South East. Loss making internal Scottish Region services such as Glasgow-Aberdeen remained with Provincial Services, but would be marketed under the InterCity brand name.
Product reshaping was to improve ancillary services such as telephone information, car parking and seat reservations. Catering was to be revamped; what was the point of serving 10-15 lunches at £7 per head when 200 people were queueing at the buffet counter? Punctuality, cleanliness and facilities for infants were all due for attention. More cross-London services would be provided using the West London Line and (possibly) the Snow Hill tunnel. Parkways were to be extended in the Western Region and perhaps elsewhere. The Executive concept was submerged in favour of a relaunched Pullman title, and early results suggested a 20% gain in patronage

Left:
For its final year, the 'Manchester Pullman' was bedecked in the new InterCity livery and extensively promoted.

Right:
The 'Manchester Pullman' was withdrawn in May after 19 years of service using the original Pullman cars supplied at the time of the West Coast electrification to London in 1966. In 1984 the service had been relaunched: 'The "Manchester Pullman" is a premier class train in the grand tradition of Pullman travel . . . each car has been tastefully refurbished with a pleasant decor and the Pullman tradition of naming each car revived.' In its former guise, No 86.230 *The Duke of Wellington* approaches Ardwick with the down morning service from Euston in August 1983.
Kim Fullbrook

for the Yorkshire Pullman introduced in May. Traction policy envisaged a 60-70 strong fleet of Class 91 InterCity 225 locomotives for the ECML and WCML capable of 140mph, hauling or propelling new design Mk 4 coaches each 23m long (but with tilting versions up to 6deg for the West Coast only).

A new fares strategy introduced in May 1985 aimed to price nearer production costs, but also according to what the traffic would bear at different times of the day and week. First class capacity was to be examined; as many travellers have guessed, first class coaches account for 30% of rolling stock but only 15% of revenue.

Resource management was aimed at improving rolling stock utilisation. Train lengths were planned to increase to cope with 4% higher passenger levels, compensating for a 10% reduction in train mileage after a 26% drop since 1980. High Speed Trains on the ECML would incorporate nine trailers thanks to new construction, and WR train sets would have eight. A new Charter train unit was also set up.

Below:
The new livery as applied to No 86.231 *Starlight Express*, a name chosen also for a new London-Dumfries-Glasgow overnight service. That train conveys Mk 3 sleeping cars, first class seating with dimmed lighting (Nightrider facility), refreshment car and video coach.
John Glover

London Regional Transport

London Regional Transport came into being on 29 June 1984, with the duty 'to provide or secure the provision of public passenger transport services for Greater London'. Whilst an arm's length relationship was to be established with its own subsidiaries London Underground Railways and London Buses, there was to be closer cooperation with British Rail. Now under the direct control of the Secretary of State for Transport,both organisations were told that it was the government's intention that there should be a common framework of objectives. These were, in particular, 'a better match between demand for services and their supply; better interchanges between rail, bus and Underground; better coordinated services, route timetables and information to passengers, helped by through ticketing and Travelcard arrangements; no wasteful duplication of services provided; and innovation in improving services, facilities and value for money of public transport in London, involving the private sector where appropriate'.

A number of areas were identified for special consideration, including the development of service standards on the Underground, joint marketing, common ticketing and information systems, measures to foster easier travel for the frail and disabled, comprehensive fares systems; and investment for improving interchanges.

To aid fares integration, Capitalcard was introduced in January 1985. Valid for periods between a week and a year, Capitalcard

Below:
London Regional Transport's Business Plan disclosed that Underground train mileage would increase marginally in 1985/86 but that the main aim was to maintain service quality. There were to be no closures. Work on conversion to Driver Only Operation would continue, and station staff would be more effectively deployed. A crew operated train of '1973' stock on the Piccadilly line calls at Hammersmith; the most significant service change of the year would be the opening of the Heathrow Terminal 4 extension, though this was later postponed until 1986. *John Glover*

allows travel in two or more adjoining fares zones by British Rail, Underground and bus. The more difficult problem of through ticketing on ordinary tickets remained to be achieved.

The Government's intentions for London were significantly different from those proposed for the remainder of the country, including the Passenger Transport Executive areas. Here it was argued that such coordination of bus services as was necessary would be carried out through market forces; the effect on local railways generally and on all locally funded capital improvement schemes became the subject of intense debate.

Below left:
As part of the joint review of services, Bakerloo Line Underground services were again extended to Harrow and Wealdstone. A Class 501 British Rail train overtakes a '1938' stock train in the turnback sidings. The joint approach was further advanced in January by the introduction of Capitalcard, a period ticket which could be used on all public transport in London. *John Glover*

Below:
London Regional Transport was pressed to improve the interchange arrangements between all modes of transport in the London area. At Greenford, the long-standing cross-platform facility allows interchange between the BR Ealing Broadway service and the Central Line. The Class 121 unit succeeded in beating the '1962' stock train out of the station after passengers had transferred; the general air of efficiency was enhanced by the immediate return of the starting signal to danger.
John Glover

Electrification Progress

Bottom:
The development of the 'Wonderworld' entertainment complex at Corby was one of the factors which led to the inclusion of Bedford-Kettering-Corby into the electrification programme for the London and South East sector. There are no passenger rail services to Corby, and the Rail Link bus service from Kettering was withdrawn through lack of patronage. No 47.265 heads north at Sharnbrook between Bedford and Wellingborough on the slow lines. *Michael J. Collins*

The big electrification news was the approval given for the East Coast electrification by the Government on 27 July 1984. Chairman Bob Reid called it the most important investment decision for British Rail in over 25 years. However, the £306million cost was to be funded internally, by British Rail reaching revenue targets and achieving cost reductions. Expenditure was broken down as follows: Infrastructure £170million, Motive power £62million, Locomotive hauled coaches and multiple units £74million. Benefits were the savings in maintenance costs (around 60%), reduced fuel costs (20% less) and much improved reliability. (50-70% better). The existing HST fleet would be moved to other services.

In addition to the 1985 completed schemes to Ipswich, between Dalston Western Junction and North Woolwich, and from Rock Ferry to Hooton, authorisation had been obtained for the following schemes by the middle of the year:

Scheme	Route	Route Miles	Cost	Completion
ER London area	Wickford-Southminster Romford-Upminster	20	£3m	May 1986
Hastings	Tonbridge-St Leonards	31	£24m	May 1986
Anglia West	Bishops Stortford-Cambridge	25	£10m	May 1987
Ayrshire	Paisley-Ayr/Ardrossan/Largs	50	£70m	May 1987
Anglia East	Colchester-Harwich/Norwich	75	£58m	May 1987
East Coast Main Line	Hitchin-Peterborough	44	£306m	May 1987
	Peterborough-Leeds	109		October 1989
	Doncaster-Edinburgh	237		May 1991
East Grinstead	South Croydon-East Grinstead	18	£8m	December 1987
Snow Hill	Farringdon-Blackfriars	1	£2m	May 1988
Cross-London	Camden Road-Stratford etc.	6	£12m	October 1988

Further schemes were at various stages of preparation/submission:

Scheme	Route	Route Miles
Strathclyde	Muirend-East Kilbride (via new curve)	6
Blackpool	Manchester-Blackpool North	49
Ringway	Manchester Airport (from Styal line-new construction)	1
Liverpool	Liverpool-Earlestown	13
Windermere	Oxenholme-Windermere	10
Corby	Bedford-Kettering-Corby	32
Dorset	Branksome-Weymouth	32

Below:
Electrification of the East Coast line was not expected to bring to an end the use of HSTs north of Doncaster, as North-East-South-West services would still be projected under the wires. The 07.05 from Cardiff Central crosses the High Level Bridge at Newcastle and will terminate here.
John Glover

Above:
Crew familiarisation runs in East Anglia preceded the introduction of electric traction to Ipswich in May. No 86.324 passes Hatfield Peverel with the 11.02 Thornton Fields-Colchester. *Michael J. Collins*

Right:
No 310.091 was ready for anything with Oxenholme displayed on its blind whilst stabled at Bletchley. Excursions of EMUs over Shap are virtually unknown, but a fill-in electrification scheme on the Windermere branch could eliminate unproductive diesel unit mileage north of Preston. With the reinstatement of a run-round loop at the terminus, electric loco-hauled services could be restored at minimal cost. *John Glover*

Corporate Plan

Four messages about the prospects for the future of the railway industry emerged from the Corporate Plan late in 1984. Provided British Rail continued to carry out the action plans they had set themselves, said Sir Robert Reid, who received a knighthood in the 1985 Queen's Birthday Honours:

'We will continue to receive Government support at a level which enables us to plan an expanding business on a network only slightly smaller than the present one.

'We will continue to make sensible economies in the size of our workforce and tackle the recruitment of some 25,000 people to replace those retiring or moving to other jobs.

'We will continue to earn the money to invest some £2.2billion in modernising the system over the next five years.

'We will continue with our drive to improve service to the customer by better deployment of staff, by better information services, better training for staff dealing with customer needs, and by achieving the defined standards of quality of service.

Above all, we will retain the confidence of the customer and the taxpayer, and this secures our future.'

Left:
Freight sector strategy in the Corporate Plan included the maximum worthwhile development of trainload traffic, amongst which it was thought that aggregates would show significant increases. At Kennet Redland siding, No 45.003 was pictured with the 09.48 twice weekly train from Mountsorrell.
John C. Baker

Left:
Customer care received major attention in a wish to ensure that maximum opportunity was taken to relate the products offered to the market. The neat and tidy appearance of the far from modern Kirkham & Wesham station, albeit on a brilliant summer's day, gave credence to the admen's slogan that 'We're getting there'. No 47.413 arrives with a train for Blackpool North.
Les Nixon

1985

Top right:
May 1985 saw the completion of the track remodelling and resignalling at Exeter St Davids, and the elimination of the semaphores. No 47.440 arrives with the 09.20 Liverpool Lime Street-Penzance. *Geoff Gillham*

Above right:
The National Union of Mineworkers' strike ground painfully into 1985. British Rail estimated their revenue losses as around £5million a week, but about a quarter of this was due to railwaymen blacking traffic on offer. The long term effect on Railfreight would depend on how much traffic was regained when the strike was over. In happier times, one of the Roumanian built Class 56 locomotives No 56.019 draws into Markham Colliery ready to load its MGR hoppers. *Chris Davis*

Right:
The withdrawal of the last of the 2,000hp Class 40 locomotives took place in 1985. First entering service in 1958, they were based in all Regions except the Southern and the Western. In their day, they were regularly used for the top main line expresses. In more recent years they were used mainly on freight duties; No 40.088 takes the line for the north at Newcastle with the Haverton Hill-Leith ammonia train.
John Glover

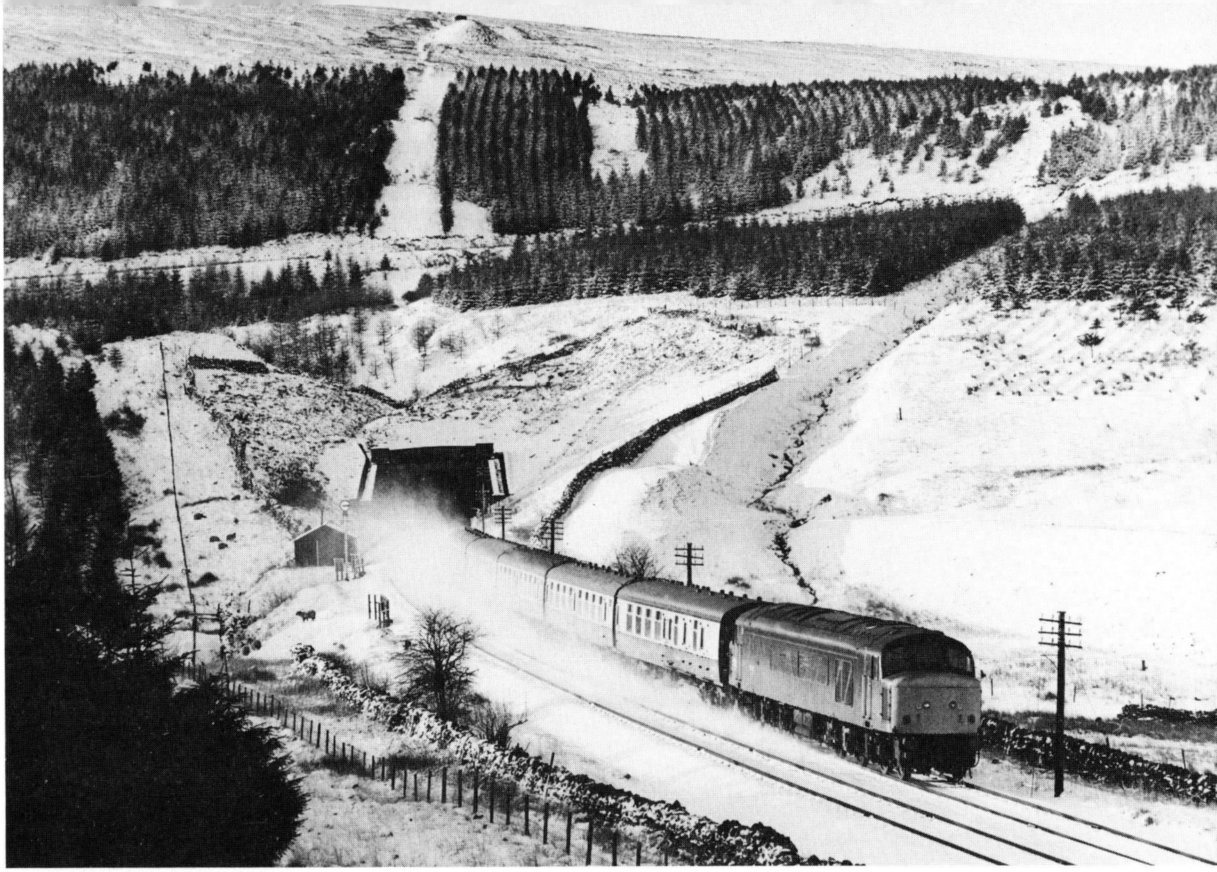

The Settle & Carlisle line, by general consent, is the most impressive scenic railway in England. Built primarily as a competitive venture by the Midland Railway, intermediate traffic has always been sparse; its main value has been as a diversionary route. By 1985 all except local passenger traffic had been accommodated elsewhere; the TUCC closure procedure had been started, and this would lead in due course to a Ministerial decision on its future.

Above:
At the north end of Blea Moor tunnel in January, No 45.101 is in charge of the 09.07 Leeds-Carlisle. *Les Nixon*

Left:
In March, No 47.410 nears Birkett tunnel with a southbound 'Scout Special No 2'. *Les Nixon*

Above:
A Class 47 is in charge of the 10.40 Carlisle-Leeds as it heads south through Crosby Garrett in November.
John Whitehouse

Right:
West Yorkshire's policy of opening low cost paytrain stations and investing in the Class 141 diesel units is seen in this picture of Deighton station east of Huddersfield, opened in 1982. All that is required is the provision of platforms, shelters, lighting and access; maintenance costs are minimal. West Yorkshire had an extensive programme, and similar developments were taking place elsewhere in the country. *Les Nixon*

APPENDICES

Right:
Another class which became extinct in 1980 was the GEC-built Class 84 ac locomotives. Despite appearances to the contrary, a commendably clean No 84.002 was not hauling the 'Manchester Pullman' out of Piccadilly, but merely removing the empty stock of the down morning service from Euston to the sidings.
Geoff Dowling

1. British Rail Traffic Statistics 1978-83 & 1984/85

	1978	1979	1980	1981	1982	1983	15 months to 31 March 1985	12 months to 31 March 1985
Passenger journeys (millions)								
Ordinary fares	430.2	438.9	429.0	395.9	361.9	386.4	473.7	
Season tickets	293.6	297.3	331.2	322.5	268.2	308.8	383.5	n/a
Total passenger journeys (millions)	723.8	736.2	760.1	718.4	630.1	695.2	857.2	700.7
Passenger miles total (millions)	19,100	19,900	18,800	18,500	16,900	18,300	22,600	18,500
Average distance per passenger journey (miles)	26.4	27.0	24.7	25.8	26.8	26.4	26.4	26.4
Freight traffic (million tonnes)								
Coal and coke	94.0	93.5	94.4	95.1	88.4	87.9	31.3	
Iron and steel	24.7	25.1	12.9	18.2	14.3	16.1	14.7	
Other	44.3	43.1	38.9	33.8	32.7	33.9	42.6	n/a
Freightliner	7.5	7.6	7.5	7.0	6.5	7.2	8.2	
Total freight traffic (million tonnes)	170.5	169.3	153.4	154.2	141.9	145.1	96.8	68.0
Freight tonne miles total (millions)	12,416	12,361	10,961	10,877	9,867	10,653	9,844	7,476
Average length of haul (miles)	72.82	73.00	71.41	70.55	69.53	73.40	101.70	109.94
Loaded wagons forwarded (millions)	7.0	6.7	5.9	5.7	5.0	5.1	3.3	2.3

Source: British Railways Board Annual Report and Accounts. The accounting year was changed to 1 April–31 March with effect from 1984/85; consequently the statistics for that year cover a 15 month period.

Right:
The new Sandwell & Dudley station got off to an embarrassing start when the driver of the 06.36 Wolverhampton-Euston forgot to stop on the first day and left the assembled company behind. Of longer term interest, the May 1984 timetable also saw the first through workings of HSTs under the wires to Manchester and Liverpool. The 06.14 Bristol Temple Meads-Manchester Piccadilly arrives at Sandwell and Dudley in August.
John Glover

2. British Rail Assets as at 1 January 1978-1984 and as at 31 March 1985

	1978	1979	1980	1981	1982	1983	1984	1985
Locomotives diesel	3,290	3,268	3,261	3,078	2,864	2,750	2,603	2,467
electric	320	312	310	301	267	266	247	244
APT power cars	—	2	5	6	6	6	6	6
HST power cars	76	109	136	142	181	197	197	197
Passenger carriages								
Locomotive hauled	6,086	5,967	5,885	5,567	5,070	4,468	4,059	3,869
Diesel multiple-unit	3,313	3,293	3,284	3,257	3.096	2,917	2,703	2,617
Electric multiple-unit	7,343	7,341	7,456	7,558	7,306	7,276	7,306	7,078
APT	—	6	15	30	30	30	30	30
HST	302	421	533	630	664	709	709	709
Non passenger carrying coaching vehicles	4,838	4,430	4,336	4,026	2,796	2,228	2,156	2,130
Freight vehicles	166,935	150,371	137,589	119,507	87,955	71,452	54,510	45,174
Brake vans etc	3,797	3,698	3,845	2,946	2,380	1,466	1,121	880
Private owner freight vehicles licenced to run on BR tracks	18.527	18.438	18.676	18.752	17,244	16,408	15,902	14,842
Total seats/berths in passenger carriages (thousands)	1,073	1,080	1,091	1,090	1,044	1,003	971	940
Total capacity of owned freight wagons (thousand tonnes)	3,563	3,315	3,095	2,769	2,149	1,831	1,488	1,304
Passenger stations	2,358	2,364	2,365	2,366	2,361	2,369	2,363	2,376
Route open for traffic (miles)								
Passenger traffic only	678	698	724	717	719	721	736	878
Passenger and freight	8,278	8,247	8,231	8,227	8,230	8,209	8,196	8,010
Freight only	2,212	2,178	2,065	2,020	1,882	1,776	1,609	1,553
Total route open (miles)	11,168	11,123	11,020	10,964	10,831	10,706	10,541	10,441
of which, electrified,								
ac overhead	1,156	1,125	1,125	1,125	1,188	1,204	1,204	1,238
dc overhead	77	71	71	71	17	17	16	nil
dc third rail	1,108	1,113	1,114	1,114	1,112	1,111	1,110	1,122

Source: British Railways Board Annual Report and Accounts

3. British Rail Business Performance Indicators 1980-1984/85

Total Railways		**1980**	**1981**	**1982**	**1983**	**1984/85**	**1984/85 adjusted***
Total receipts per train mile	£	7.32	7.21	6.94	7.16	6.53	7.22
Total operations and train provision expenses per train mile	£	2.48	2.54	2.61	2.50	2.44	2.42
Operations control expenses per train mile	£	0.67	0.69	0.72	0.61	0.65	0.64
Train maintenance expenses per train mile	£	2.06	2.02	2.17	1.94	1.85	1.82
Terminals expenses per train mile	£	1.11	1.05	1.07	1.02	1.05	1.04
Track and associated structural expenses per train mile	£	1.70	1.68	1.86	1.87	1.94	1.90
Signalling and telecommunications expenses per train mile	£	0.57	0.58	0.61	0.56	0.64	0.63
Management expenses per train mile	£	n/a	n/a	n/a	0.55	0.55	0.54
Total operating expenses per train mile	£	10.51	10.73	11.57	10.80	11.13	10.97
Train miles per member of staff (total staff productivity)	No	1,570	1,597	1,495	1,686	1,713	1,748
Revenue per £1,000 gross paybill costs	£	1,465	1,398	1,262	1,402	1,245	1,396
Train miles per train crew member (train crew productivity)	No	7,244	7,478	6,947	7,898	7,880	8,045
Train miles per single track mile	000s	12.8	12.6	11.3	12.5	12.2	12.4
Train miles per locomotive/HST set	000s	53.4	55.2	51.1	57.1	55.3	57.7

All prices converted to 1984/85 price levels. The last column adjusts the actual indicators for 1984/85 for the effects of the coal strike, to demonstrate the underlying trends.

Source: British Railways Board Annual Report and Accounts

Left:
The Class 50 refurbishment programme was intended to provide a long term improvement in performance. Work was concentrated in three areas: the removal of redundant equipment, the provision of an efficient ventilation and filtration system, and a full rehabilitation and refurbishing of electrical and electronic components with technical updating. Visually prominent features are the headlight and, from the seventh to be dealt with No 50.023 *Howe*, repainting in the new livery. No 50.023 leaves Oxford for Paddington. *John Glover*